Sex and the Gospel

Sex and the Gospel

*A Brief Declaration of Human Sexuality and How It Is
Understood in the Light of Lordship, Law, and Salvation*

JASON TACKETT

RESOURCE *Publications* · Eugene, Oregon

SEX AND THE GOSPEL
A Brief Declaration of Human Sexuality and How It is Understood in the
Light of Lordship, Law, and Salvation

Resource Publications
An Imprint of Wipf and Stock Publishers
199 W. 8th Ave., Suite 3
Eugene, OR 97401

www.wipfandstock.com

PAPERBACK ISBN: 979-8-3852-1918-6
HARDCOVER ISBN: 979-8-3852-1919-3
EBOOK ISBN: 979-8-3852-1920-9
05/03/24

All Scripture references use the King James Version of the Bible.

Contents

Preface

THE PURPOSE OF THIS humble work is not to provide an exhaustive volume that will answer all possible questions. Nor is it an attempt to be witty and insightful about any particular aspect of the subject matter. Nor is it an attempt to address the sprit of the age, the zeitgeist, or provide a defense for why Christians believe any presently stated proposition or its negation. This short work is not an attempt to grandstand on any current issue or moral question and it does not seek to push a political agenda. Instead, this work seeks to provide only a general primer to the subject of sex and sexuality from a Christian perspective. It is putting forth an offensive front, a declaration of what Christian doctrine is. It is the aim of this discourse to provide a foundation for those who come after me, whereby they can begin to construct a coherent structure of practice.

This work will, by its nature, leave areas of the subject untouched in order to focus on what this author feels is of first importance. The subject of sex is not something divorced from the truth, goodness, and beauty that our God has bestowed on this world. It reflects those things. And it is not unrelated to the gospel that is the power of God unto salvation. I pray that it will serve to correct those that see sex as a matter independent from the gospel and subjective in its meaning. I pray that it will be a starting point for seeing God and Christ in the things that are made. And I commend it to the conscience of the reader to see the necessity of glorifying God in all things.

For Christ alone,
Jason Tackett

Introduction

Sex and the Gospel

"Flee fornication. Every sin that a man doeth is without the body; but he that committeth fornication sinneth against his own body. What? know ye not that your body is the temple of the Holy Ghost which is in you, which ye have of God, and ye are not your own? For ye are bought with a price: therefore glorify God in your body, and in your spirit, which are God's." First Corinthians 6:18-20

WHY THE SUBJECT OF SEX SO IMPORTANT:

Thinking in the terms of antithesis is the metaphysical and moral necessity for all. There are two, and all is not one. The embarrassing history of human philosophy is the repeated and failed attempts to insert synthesis (making two one) into the created order; a unifying concept that explains all things, all while denying there is knowledge of a created order. One of the ancient Greeks would say all is fire and another one would say all is water. 2,500 years have passed, and the contemporary metaphysician would say all is random quantum fluctuations. Both equally destroys reality by an insertion of a false synthesis that denies the truths of God. If there is to be any unity it must come first from this truth; God is God, and we (as well as all other things) are not God. His Logos is the foundation of all things and not chaos. This alone is a truth that brings unity to all particular things. There is one God and all things that are outside of God are subject to that God.

What is clear from the portion of Scripture quoted above (I Cor 6:18-20) is that we all clearly belong under the Sovereignty of another. That truth shapes us wholly. We are not free, therefore, to compartmentalize our lives in any way away from that truth. There is no autonomy from this blessed rule over us and there is no place in our lives over which God lacks complete authority. What we do with our outward bodies is just as much under the Sovereignty of another as what we do in our innermost spiritual life. There is no space in our life to speak of anything about us as being ours to do with as we please. Our physical reality did not arise out of chaos and cannot be lived in chaos. It exists by His Logos. These are the terms in which the apostle spoke to us about the subject of sex, and it will be the ground of our understanding moving forward.

Why does this matter to you? Sex in our culture seems to be an individualistic and self-contained activity. It is a subjective matter that, we are told, cannot be governed by anything outside of the subject. Why should we try to speak about it in real and objective universal terms? Why should we be critical of it and speak of it in a way that possibly runs afoul of our neighbor? If we speak of it at all, do we, as we are said to do, attempt to take this all-important freedom from the individual? Are we puritanical despots for declaring that sex must be governed by the truth of God?

From the Christian perspective alone the importance of the issue can be seen. Why is it necessary for us to speak about it? One reason why sex matters is because it represents one of the greatest challenges to the faithful. The Christian faces this question increasingly as the culture around them runs with eagerness to the most extreme forms of depravity and demands that the Christian accepts and celebrates those expressions. This immediately places us at odds with our culture and makes sex the staging ground for a great assault on the faith of the Christian. The outside world, who views the Christian teaching on sex to be outmoded and contrary to its contemporary mores, are ready to make us the point of ridicule and persecution based solely on this issue alone. Lot had a place at the gates of Sodom till he called their sinful sexual practices wicked. John the Baptist could freely preach in Judea until he spoke about the sex life of the king.

The Sexual Revolution of the 1960's has literally reshaped the culture in which we live. What was it revolting from or against? In a sense, that generation was rejecting the mores of the generation that preceded it. There was a certain level of hypocrisy that was mixed in with that former generation. And the hippie generation, as Francis Shaffer pointed out, saw the vanity of the pursuit of personal peace and affluence, and rightfully rejected it. Added to that, they saw the hypocrisy of their fathers, which was often couched in Christian language, at the base of issues like racism, inter-racial marriages, and such like. The rejection of the vanity and hypocrisy of the preceding generation entered the realm of sexual ethics, influenced by an undercurrent of New Left ideology; an ideology which reinterpreted Marxists terms of class warfare to embrace identity politics in terms of oppressed racial and sexual minorities in revolution against a dominant systematic oppression. And this prevailing new view of evolving sexual ethics built on intellectuals of the stature of Kinsey, Freud, Jung, Joyce, and many others went mainstream. A rebellion against the mores of the previous generation ended up not just repudiating the vanity and hypocrisy of the previous generation but aimed at overthrowing the idea of the God of the Scriptures and replacing it with its own ethics and gods, with sex being the central sacrament of its faith.

Such a revolution has successfully redefined how all of our culture sees sex conceptually. One can no longer disagree with someone about the ethics of a person without falling into the category of one that oppresses others; one that is the beneficiary of the dominant class that systemically oppresses the minority classes. The virtue of the New Left will not allow for any moral reasoning to escape the status of oppression, which is seen as an attempt to enslave those who hold to their sacraments. It is our view of sex that will likely soon make us enemies of the state and society at large and will be the reason church doors are boarded shut or razed to the ground. Make no error here, sex is an idol shaped and worshiped by a society opposed to our God. Idolatry is at the heart of the sexual mores of culture and if we are to serve our God rightly, we must adhere to His first command to have no other gods before Him.

A second reason why the subject of sex is important is that sex represents one of the greatest stumbling blocks in the way of professing believers. Clearly seeing a coming tide of opposition, professing Christian churches are ready to compromise, and even abandon what God has clearly spoken, in order to shelter themselves from attack, ridicule, or, worse yet, to win acceptance from the society that has rejected their God. But, in doing so, they compromise the very truth itself. It is, therefore, important for us to hold fast the form of truth we have received (II Tim 1:13). A church fractured in the area of truth cannot minister in a world of falsehood.

And, further, the subject of sex is connected with our glorious hope in God. If Paul taught that the man/wife relationship is a picture of Christ and His church and therefore connected to our hope of Him (Eph 5:22-32), then we cannot abandon the truth of it without affecting that hope as well. The recent advent of deconstructing one's faith, which is often ending in people openly apostatizing from Christ, inevitably ends with people citing sexuality as one of their chief contentions against the God of the Scriptures. The road to sexual licentiousness is like Dante's Inferno, with words writ large over it, "Abandon all hope, ye who enter." We cannot comprise it, without losing what is essential to our faith. It is these greater points that this humble work seeks to illuminate.

A greater reason for the importance of the subject of sex is that it is one of the areas of greatest personal danger for the Christian. We should flee fornication or sexual immorality. We can all personally fall into this sin. There are none too holy to fall, too pious to bend. We have all known people, sometimes people who had been faithful for years, that have fallen into grievous sexual sin. And as such, the Christian is capable of being affected by the culture around them. They can, in eagerness of rationalizing and justifying their own desires or the desires of others, jettison sound biblical teaching for the spirit of the age.

What is needed is what is true to guide them and not what is felt emotionally. To say, "I want what I want" is no reason to pursue it or believe it would be a good thing to do. Sexual sin can bring on us great guilt, not just sins against our soul but against our body. And this error can keep us from glorifying our God holistically in our bodies and in our spirits, from worshiping in spirit and in truth (I Cor 6:19, 20, John 4:24). If we long for true worship, we must not allow this area of our life to be untouched by its Lord. To embrace a religion that is only found in the fuzzy area of feelings and not in the real world of the works of our bodies is to have divided loyalty toward our Lord. We cannot serve two Lord's without eventually hating the true one (Matt 6:24).

THE METHOD OF THIS BOOK:

This work will not be an attempt to lay out a how to guide for sex, something resembling a high school health class from a Christian perspective, complete with anatomical references and uncomfortable inuendo. Nor is it the aim of this work to catalog all possible sins of a sexual nature. In fact, little will be said about any specific sin. There will not be an attempt to give theological meaning to any act by way of picture or allegory, above what is directly proclaimed by Scripture. Nor will there be an attempt to bind the conscience of any reader about what is or is not acceptable in the confines of God-given boundaries. This work is only intended to be a general introduction and overview of sexuality as a biblical concept, a concept under Lordship. I am not trying to say what others have said better or to draw out profound insights of practical psychology. If that is what the reader desires, this is not the book to read. The goal here is to glorify the Lord as Lord in regard to the subject of sexuality. This short treatise is simply trying to offer a Christian lens or perspective from which one can view and evaluate sexuality in its acts and attitudes.

Therefore, to repeat what was asserted in the preface, this will not be apologetic in any classical sense. This is simply a declaration of the God that I actually believe in and about the world I actually believe He created. It is an apologetic in that sense alone, a reason given for the hope that lies in me, with meekness and fear (I Pet 3:15). It is the God of the Scriptures that is glorified by right belief, right behavior, and the declaration of the truth; I wish now to honor Him alone. I will declare it and you are free to judge its merits. The goal of this humble work is to present God, His nature and His will, clearly and without compromise. Then the goal will be to give a defense of that truth to those who wish to deny Him.

On the subject of sex, the reality that God is Lord over all, that He has spoken on this subject, and that those who refuse to hear Him and glorify Him in it are opposed to Him is too often overlooked. Glorifying Him therefore is the paramount concern here. Therefore, I won't argue up to God then back down to the subject of sex, that is the classical and evidentiary approach to apologetics. Instead, I will speak to the conscience of the reader from the Scriptures about the God they know is there. God must be proclaimed, not as a probability but as a truth.

What I mean by this not being an apologetic is worth noting in a fuller summary. If we were to deviate into an argument and begin to try to produce evidence for the God of the Scriptures, I am afraid we would be fighting a battle that is unwinnable (even if it would also be unlosable as well). Is there evidence at each point of questioning that we can argue? There is a plenitude of evidence. This is what evidential apologetics (which has its place) looks like when declaring sin to the sinner.

The first question asked, "Is there a God?" It is a question that divides between the worldview of atheism and theism. Can we produce compelling evidence that this question is more likely than not answered in favor of theism and shows that a god probably exists? Of Course! But we do so by giving one the false impression that they can hide from God because He is only a probability, or that He might even be one of many, that He may be possibly indifferent, or that He may be only an abstract concept. There is nothing there that moves the conscience

The second question asked, "Is that God personal or impersonal?" Surely there is a plethora of what can be set forth in our arguments as evidence of the personal nature of God. No doubt we can tout that theism has superior explanatory power over pantheism. But we have not yet spoken anything to the hearts of the people before us. Worse, we allow them to cling to a false hope that they are not accountable.

The third question asked, "Is that God presently working in His creation or not?" Is God deistic or theistic? There is evidence that we can put forth here as well. Every contingent thing could have been otherwise and only is because an active and powerful mind has made it thus. But, in all our efforts, we have not yet even touched on the real issue. Also, counterproductively, we allowed the hearer to cling to a small hope that God is indifferent to what they do, just somewhere out there beyond us. We have not even got to the question of whether God has spoken.

We can win each of these arguments (or at least show our position to be just as tenable as our opponents) and yet accomplish very little. The fact is, each person we speak to is not morally neutral. They are sinners that do not desire for the God of whom we speak to exist (Rom 3:10-18). The sinner desires their sin and not their God. And those dark spots hidden deep in our unsanctified spirits are not that different. They will resist all evidence and arguments that we put forth for this very reason. So, I will not speak from an evidentiary mindset. I speak only of the God and the reality that I believe in and do so to the conscience of the reader. They may choose to retain God in their knowledge or drive Him away, but they cannot say that He was never clearly proclaimed to them.

Also, the questions above are not morally neutral questions. Our conclusions, no matter how sound, are met with spiritual and moral resistance for that reason. All know that there is a God, they suppress that knowledge, create new gods after their own desires, and pursue greater sins, including sexual sins (Rom 1:18-28). They do not want God and will maintain their systems of thought to keep from having to admit that they must yet stand before Him as sinners. This is so, especially, if that system of thought allows them to have a sense of godlike autonomy over their bodies and spirits absent any real moral imperative from a God that has spoken and will judge.

Therefore, the task before the Christian is not primarily to argue from evidence but to declare the truth of this God that all already know in their conscience to be there. We need to show them the folly of their sin (and remind ourselves as well of that same folly), and from there alone can we declare the riches of the glory of the gospel that rescues from sin. Until the hearer sees clearly that all that they do *counts*, is meaningful, only because they are *accountable* to the one true God, nothing we say will convince them. They will only go about ignorantly thinking that they can autonomously decide for themselves whether God is and whether He has any authority.

The rationalism of the world, which ultimately is irrationality, is not the wisdom of the knowledge of God. Their irrationality ends with no real purpose for sex, or any meaning outside of the fleeting experience. Their rejection of God is their rejection of everything reasonable and rational, Chaos being their ultimate instead of Logos. When they speak of truth, they are already engaging in the arena that declares loudly that this God is there. When they indignantly speak of justice or morality, they have tossed their hat in the ring where they must contend with His reality, a reality which if pondered would shake them to the core of their conscience. When they speak of beauty, they touch on that which is only because this God is. God is the necessary ground of these things. Without the God of the Scriptures there is no teleology or design ultimately at which we can stand in awe of or be thankful for. They cannot escape the one they reject because of their sin. And sex is not absent from truth, goodness, and beauty which flows from God and screams out to our consciences that we must answer to Him for what we do with such a gift.

The topic of sex and sexuality, as a creature of God is no different than any other concept or creature of God. Can we offer sound arguments for the maintaining of sexual morality? Of course, we can. But we will not spend a great deal of time, if any, doing so here. We can argue how it is pragmatic to maintain Christian ethics regarding sexuality and show how destructive it can be to breach these ethics both individually and socially. Sound sexual morals would doubtless reduce crime, prison recidivism, psychosis, suicidal ideation and attempts, feelings of low self-worth, etc. But pragmatism does not convince anyone of their need for God. Christian sexual ethics making one healthier and happier is an empty promise to one who is tempted with the sales line that says sexual sin will do the same. All the evidence in the world will not gain us a hearing in our culture. They hate Christian ethics regarding sex and sexuality because they speak so loudly of the reality of God and sin, topics they are eager to avoid. That is the obstacle that stands in the way of the Christian having dialogue with the world. If they hated Christ, they will also hate the ones who speak in the name of Christ (John 15;18). If they put Him to death, they will eventually do so to all who want to follow Him. Or, as I saw lately on a protester sign held by one advocating for unfettered sexual liberty, "If Christ comes back, kill him again!"

Paul clearly teaches that we should behave ethically in this matter of sexuality because we honor God holistically with our bodies and spirits. We are to declare that. So, this work will be short and simple. It will first present to the reader the antitheses of truth that places the Christian in opposition to the sinful world. Our God created all divisions in reality. From the first chapter of our Scriptures our Lord made distinctions and separations in this world that we may know the difference between this and that. When we approach sex from the biblical point of view, these antitheses must be reckoned with if we wish to hold fast to the truth. Once these antitheses are recognized, we will attempt to solve the antitheses that place humanity in opposition to the Lord of all. Sex answers deeper questions that are far more fulfilling than the empty teaching of the value free, meaning and purpose free, sexuality that is peddled by our culture like parade candy. Sex is not an idol to worship but, indeed, in it we may worship our Lord in spirit and in truth (John 4:24).

Part 1

Sex in Terms of Antithesis

The Ontology of Sex
Antithesis 1: The Lord and His Creation

"Ye are my witnesses, saith the Lord, and my servant whom I have chosen: that ye may know and believe me, and understand that I am he: before me there was no God formed, neither shall there be after me. I, even I, am the Lord; and beside me there is no savior." Isaiah 43:10, 11

"I am the Lord, and there is none else, there is no God beside me: I girded thee, though thou hast not known me: That they may know from the rising of the sun, and from the west, that there is none beside me. I am the Lord, and there is none else. I form the light, and create darkness: I make peace, and create evil: I the Lord do all these things." - Isaiah 45:5–7

HOW WE APPROACH THE subject of sex has everything to do with how we approach the subject of God. The former is not inseparable or independent from the latter. And everything about the first is fully informed by the second. To drive the idea of God out is to leave sex as a subject without form and void, a meaningless tome of pretended significance, Chaos without telos (the immediate product of Logos). Darwinian philosophy is often misunderstood as simply teaching gradual development of life over time. Such philosophies in the day of Darwin were plenteous. The crux of Darwinian philosophy is that there is no telos, no purpose, in anything, for there is no God to direct and give anything purpose.

All there is in Darwinian philosophy is blind chance and therefore there can be no meaning. Nothing in nature is as it is because some purpose was given to it. Randomness does not give meaning, only the mind and will of God does so. Meaning comes from the one that first spoke and all things flowed from His Logos with purposes that only come from Him. Behind the reality of sex is the one that says, "I am the Lord . . . there is no other . . . and I gave all things their significance." That was the plain declaration of the prophet (Isa 43:10, 11, 45:5–7).

We start then with the ontological question of what sex is. In short, it is a creature; created, defined, confined, and given to man (in man's context) for purposes that God alone has declared. No individual or collective of men can give ontological significance to sexuality. In a further point of brevity, sex is a creature of God over which God is Lord. Those are heavy words that are hard for men to swallow, but they are nonetheless true. As Lord, God controls it, He has absolute authority over it, and is always present to judge it. The ability to create, to control, to define, or to evaluate sexuality is outside of the capacity of mankind. Unless we see the truth of His Lordship first, everything else we have to say about sex is vanity. The fear of the Lord is the starting point of all our knowledge (Prov 1:7).

Again, if we preach sexual purity, that one ought to be pure, for the purpose of achieving better social, political, personal, psychological, or emotional outcomes, then we preach vanity. Not that sexual purity cannot and does not produce those things, but those are periphery to our understanding. Sex has its Lord. Such an approach of not declaring His Lordship but speaking only of its practical outcomes, treats sex as if it was an autonomous thing in and of itself, instead of it being a creature of God. Sexual purity should be sought because God is Lord over it and, therefore, defines it by His authority. And our use of it is accountable or answerable to Him.

By way of analogy, sex is God's country, His land, over which He is Lord. He rules over it and has set its boundaries. If we ignore His Lordship, we do so against our own happiness and toward our own just destruction. Many years ago a young man went to a foreign country and proceeded to vandalize private property, as he felt entitled to do due to the privilege he enjoyed through his familial status in his own county. Our entire country was amazed to see that same young man judged and beaten with a cane publicly for his crimes. No amount of international politics could change his fate. He failed to understand the jurisdictional authority he was under, a jurisdictional authority that was indifferent to all the perceived status he thought he had. Similarly, if we go about behaving as if we have no Lord here and now, in our daily context, we possibly run toward the same foolish end as that young man did.

The easiest thing to do in this work is to speak with the voice of dominant culture. But we have already ran afoul of culture by invoking Lordship as important to the subject of sexuality. We could easily win fans among the lost world by saying nothing meaningful about sexuality, while punching toward our fellow Christians with founded or unfounded accusations of being unloving and unbiblical. This would make us look good for a while, but such fear of disapproval from the world would make us ineffectual and eventually irrelevant. Worse, the applause we win would be short lived when they demand that we go further in affirmation of good as evil and evil as good (Isa 5:20). And each step to win their approval would become the cementing of our rebellion against God. To call Christians, who have come to believe that sex and sexuality are concepts that exist in a moral context created by God, bigoted and phobic[1] is only to swim in the current of contemporary culture. There is zero value in such a Christianity.

The dividing line is clear, the sexuality of our current culture is a unified declaration against our declaration that God is Lord in this area of life. And if this belongs not to Him, what does? What other part of your life do you believe Christ has no right to rule over? What other part of the public square do you believe should not be under His feet? The Christian confession is "Christ is Lord"

---

1. Accusatory terms that apply the idea of irrational mental illness to the outlook and belief system of an individual, which is logically fallacious and purely *ad hominem* in nature.

and the Christian politic is "He is Lord of all" (See Ps 2). And, with each compromise on this matter of Lordship, we will eventually find ourselves adrift in the boundless sea of relativistic a-morality where we deny every fundamental truth of Christ in order to win worldly applause. To see what the Christian believes as harmful to society as a whole, and to all who live out "their truth" in their sexual performances in particular, is foolish and of cowardly. But declaring God to be Lord is a message of extreme value. This enters courageously into the fray. We occupy His land, under His law, breathe His air, and owe Him all obedience. That message carries true currency for it answers to what is real.

Who do we hurt by maintaining a self-serving stance? Here is one that is trying to live out their own sexual reality, created in their own mind and in their mind answerable to no one. In doing so, that one is depressed, experiencing suicidal ideation, and even making attempts to end their own life. That same one experiences undesirable outcomes in various areas of their social and emotional life, developing a sense of hopelessness, darkness, and emptiness. To blame the Christian for these outcomes, and accuse Christian belief of causing these to perpetuate, is easy. However, it cuts the suffering person off from the only thing that could truly help them, a true currency backed by the authority of the true Sovereign. Every pill they are given to provide chemical balance, every empty affirmation that is spoken, every augment of their body to fit their mind, every act of sexual fulfillment, and every act of self medicating that dulls their senses gives them no real relief. If it does not meet their need as sinners, which only the gospel can do, then it offers them no real help, but rather encourages them in rebellion against the Lord. By our affirmation of their rebellion are we not now also co-conspirators against our Lord? We offer them play paper money that is not coined by the true Sovereign and cannot hold value outside of their delusion of being their own lord. It is cruel to give counterfeits to beggars. It is spiritual malpractice to hold the healing power of the gospel of Christ and refuse to help others with it, relying instead on the poisonous snake oils peddled by the world. What does such a nuanced and contextualized approach of Christian appeasement do but aid in keeping the lost from hearing what they need to hear, the truth of God.

Christian belief is deemed to be a thought crime, the hateful blight of society, the cause of all bad outcomes and therefore something to be driven from society for the good of the collective. The idea that the true etiology of those undesirable outcomes for the sinner is found in the denial of God as Lord, and therefore a denial of purpose to concrete reality, cannot be thought of as a viable conclusion by the advocates of rebellion. But it must here be proclaimed if we are to be true. The idea that a just recompense is distributed to those who reject God as Lord, to instead worship and serve the creature, is shunned as ignorant and unscientific by those who hate the Lord of this land. But judgment is inevitable and real to all who rebel against this world's true King. Who is warning them to flee from His just wrath to come?

Offering a message less than Lordship is untenable under our real circumstances. Those who deny Lordship will have no reservations denying lesser authorities. In fact, even trying to assign a scientific etiology to undesirable outcomes of sexual rebellion, would undercut the very ideology they want to preserve. Pragmatism tells them that something is only true if it helps them get to where they want to go, such is the contemporary voice of science. If they will not have the Lord, they will not have the order of His nature as an authority either. The cognitive dissonance of sexual rebellion knows no bounds. Foolish men are encouraged in treating their physical body as if they have no purpose or direction, except to the service of the desires of the individual mind; making it malleable plastic to be formed based on principles of self deification, a creation in the realm of one's own mind. Arguing a nameless possibility of a god somewhere, will only meet the waving hand of hypocritical skepticism that there is only an 'appearance' of design. It cannot be considered that nature has the voice of the living God behind it. There can be no norms that are not created by man, according to the rebel mind. We must then declare to all that they ought to obey the Lord and submit to His created order and normative commands.

The idea of God in the minds of those alienated from Him is what is truly at stake here. Treating a thing (e.g., the physical body) that has obvious purpose, purpose which is independent of what we think, and acting as if that purpose is not real or important, will continue to create real problems for people. Then, to go about making that thing to have a purpose that is fundamentally different from its inherent and real purpose, all because we believe that the purposes that we create in our mind are the only truth, will always end tragically. To act as if gravity has no independent reality outside of our mind will eventually lead to real injury. To act as if visual concepts such as red or green have no independent reality we all share will lead to a car crash, injury, and death. Nature, and consequently the God of nature, will always assert itself. Even the most consistent skeptics, like Hume, would not dare to try to live out their philosophies in the real created order.

So, this idea of God, the God that is presented in the Scriptures, must be set forth with its antithesis. Egalitarianism is the term I have chosen to use as that which opposes the scriptural Creator/creation antithesis. This term is chosen because it seems to be best suited to this line of thought. It may be used differently in other contexts, so we need a definition for our use. Egalitarianism is simply the belief that all things are equal, the same, and that there are no distinctions that can be made between this and that thing. It is this point of distinction that is important and controversial. When we speak of God, we speak of Him as Holy, as different, as distinct from all else (Lev 20:26, I Sam 2:2). God presents Himself in this light. He is the Creator and there is nothing that is like Him (Isa 43:10, 45:5–7). He is in a class by Himself, and all other things are not to be likened to Him.

If a view of sexuality is being built on a commitment to the doctrine of egalitarianism, that there are no real distinctions, one must contend with this fundamental distinction; God is God and nothing else that exists is God or is like God. This is what Peter Jones called the Creator/creature distinction. It is something, according to Paul, that all people intuitively know (Rom 1:18–21). All Kantian attempts to push this knowledge off into an unknowable

8

noumenal world are foolish (Ps 14:1). God has made Himself known (as the musings of Kant's moral philosophy betrayed). God is the necessary precondition for a knowable phenomenal world. Or, in a Chesterton like summary, without His sun we cannot see anything.

This distinction forms the basis of all knowledge. Aristotle may have expounded on the rules of logic (e.g., laws of identity, the excluded middle, noncontradiction, etc.) but these are only minor expressions of truth built on the Creator/creature distinction already declared by the revelation of God to Moses, the Psalmist, Job, and other biblical writers that came long before Aristotle. God declared Himself in distinction. Further than that, it is what man as a creature has always understood from the beginning. "In the beginning God . . . ." Before that beginning there was only God. Since the beginning, there is a concrete distinction between God and everything God in His wisdom and power has created outside of Himself. This is the basis for a rational understanding of truth (this is different than that), morality (this ought to be and not that), and aesthetics (this is related to and complements that). To handle an ideology of egalitarianism that fundamentally denies that this most basic distinction is real is to destroy all ability to speak of truth, goodness, and beauty. Nothing meaningful can be said about anything if there is no fundamental distinction. More basic than A is not non-A is that God is there, that He is Lord, and we and all else are not God. Pagan ideology, categories, and ethics cannot improve on the overall assumption of the Scriptures. They can lead to a pagan form of Phariseeism, which is all Aristotelian ethics is, but not to truth. He is Lord and we are not. Unlike pagan deities, God is not part of the order but the Lord over and behind the order. He created all and upholds all by His power. He is the independent reality upon which all other realities depend. Distinctions exist and are not illusions created in our minds. We are not God.

Metaphysical questions are not fruitless and dusty armchair philosophical exercises. Understanding the nature of the really real, the ultimate reality, and acting in accordance with it is of the utmost importance. God is God and not man. God is God and not creation. God is the ground upon which these things exist but His being is greater, different, and distinct from all that He made. This immediately makes egalitarianism an unthinkable ground for metaphysics, much less ethical reasoning. All is not without distinction. If it was, to paraphrase Paul, no meaning to anything could be deciphered (I Cor 14:9). We would be reduced to drooling on ourselves in a stupor.

The truth of God allows us to begin to see distinctions as a revelation of Himself in nature, the things He made. First, they reveal His power in that He alone can create that which exists outside of Himself. Created things display His eternal power and Godhood (Rom 1:18–21). Then, the variety of distinctions that encompass the beauty of our world, they speak of distinctions even in the one true God. Symbiosis, language, communication, variety, and community speak loudly of the nature of the true God, the one and the many, the Triune God of the Scriptures. Contingencies in creation speak of the delight of God who rejoiced in His freedom to make things according to His own Sovereign will. Thus, they are as they are. They could have been different than they are, but it pleased Him to make them thus. They represent the good pleasure of His will (Eph 1:11). But I am already ahead of myself.

Distinctions and separations within the created realm are made according to the wisdom and power of the Creator. Moses describes creation as God by the word of His power making separations and distinctions between things that He has caused to exist.[2] He separated light from darkness, dry land from the Sea, life from non-life, human from animal, man from woman, etc. These distinctions are the fabric of the design of creation. We on the basis of the things that are made understand the power and wisdom of God and can now make distinctions in our thought between this thing and that thing. We reason about the world because God is. Kant assumed the existence of a categorizing mind but could

---

2. The Septuagint (LXX) has strong language of the distinctions created by God between things, *ana meson,* a difference placed literally "up between" the various things.

assert the reality of nothing else. Thus, he failed by reducing truth to the psychology of the mind, our limited finite mind. Moses also asserted the existence of a categorizing mind, but it could reason only on the basis of the Creator revealing His created order to it. Reasoning is only possible if the Creator/creation distinction is true, and that the Lord has indeed made Himself known. "[The] Lord God formed every beast . . . and brought them unto Adam to see what he would call them . . ." (Gen 2:19). When we think about and experience the world created by God all distinctions are apparent. So now, there is not just a distinction between God and creation but within creation based on God acting upon it. He alone caused them to be, established their boundaries, defined them, and evaluated them. He created, made distinctions, and then called them good. This is the epistemic ground of all our knowledge of this world and ourselves in it.

What does this have to do with sex? It establishes that all distinctions are real, being the product of the creative power of the Ultimate Reality and Truth, God. It establishes that those distinctions are good distinctions within the boundaries that were created and designed by that Good and wise God. It establishes that, as a true and good creature of God, it has real beauty in its, again to use the terms used by Paul, natural or physical purposes (Rom 1:26, 27[3]). It is the product of the Source of all Beauty.

The Christian view of sex then, unless spoken ignorantly and un-scripturally, upholds the highest possible beliefs about sex. Any view of sex that deviates from the Christian view cannot uphold these superlatives. They cut sex off from truth, goodness, and beauty in the ultimate sense. They offer only a cheap counterfeit and attempt to declare that it has value and currency in the land. They offer only a view of sex that is subjectively true only for me, only good in my own eyes in that it pleases me, and only beautiful within the limited capacity of my own psychologically flawed self to give it self-contained purpose. And when we try to trade with such currency in the real world it produces only bad outcomes and

3. It is clear here that Paul asserted an authority to nature as a witness to the creation under its Lord.

merits the judgment of God. Fleeting feelings of pleasure are not good outcomes any more than a methamphetamine high is a good outcome for the addict. The rat will gorge itself on rat poison only to slowly die after its satiation.

A warning is in order at this point to address the hyper-religious. It is also definitely a sin to make distinctions in points where God has declared there to be no distinctions. If God has made from one blood all nations of men and sent the gospel out to all, then to create distinctions of mankind based on skin color or class for the purpose of respecting one over another (i.e., racism or discrimination) is evil. If God has declared all under sin, then self-righteousness is sin for it creates an arbitrary distinction not declared by God. These are distinctions men try to make that are contrary to the revealed truths of God. So, there must be a commitment to the truth as God has revealed it. Therefore, it is also sinful to approach this world from the anti-religious perspective. It is equally sinful to say that there are no distinctions when God has declared those distinctions to be. Here then is a distinction given by God, marriage is honorable but sexual immorality God will judge (Heb. 13:4). I tremble and weep for those that I love who have declared that this is not a real distinction. This is a fearful truth given by God as Lord. Sex in the eyes of God is either that which is honorable or that which is to be judged.

God is the Lord of all things, including sex. Therefore, to have truth about sex is to be fully submitted to the Lord. To have "one's own truth" contrary to the truth of God is to live a lie. One cannot deny all that the Lord does in His rule over the creature and still end up with something that is true. They are transacting with counterfeit coins. God in His Sovereign control as Lord created sex as it is. God in His Sovereign authority as Lord created all moral boundaries in regards to sex. He created it, defined it, and evaluated it (as in the creation account - He spoke and it was, He called it what it is, and He declared its goodness). God in His immanent presence as Lord judges all things. He is Lord and we are not. The "authentic self" that tries to act autonomously outside of the Lordship of God over sex will, again, only find themselves in rebellion against the Lord. For they too are under His rule (created, defined, and evaluated by Him). Being true to oneself is a misnomer. We ought rather to be true to God.

Autonomous men will grope for value in the acts that they do, while setting themselves outside of God's authority. They think they can be the evaluator of goodness and worth for themselves, only to find their beauty turned to ashes while it produces only chaos in their lives. Sex outside of real Lordship is a recipe for meaninglessness and emptiness. It does not make people whole, contrary to its advertisement, but creates a new depth of pain and sickness in them. It is not cathartic but polluting. In its zeal to escape all judgment, it trembles knowing that it is destined to be judged by its true Lord.

Sex, then, must be something subject to the Lord. This observation, however, does not answer all questions about it. But, it is the necessary first step in understanding sexuality. What one believes about sex and what one does sexually must be subject to God as Lord.

Without fear of redundancy, creating the physical world and establishing its boundaries in its distinctions, God automatically asserted His Lordship over all that is used. Those who deny that nature has real natural uses or purposes (i.e., essentialism) do so that they may suppress the idea of God's Lordship. Our culture has gone from a Kantian view, that the nature of things cannot be known, to a postmodern view, that no nature exists. Postmodernism denies the existence of any metanarrative and nature is a metanarrative that speaks of how things really are and carries ethical, metaphysical, and aesthetical authority. To view the physical world as having no teleology is to be purposefully ignorant of all that we observe, the voice of the heavens and earth giving glory to their Lord. The acorn has a purposive direction. The very cells in our body have purposive direction. The universe as a whole and in it distinctions declares the glory of God and the realm of our existence shows us His wise working (Ps 19:1). Throughout all time, day unto day, they consistently speak of the reality of the one true God (Ps 19:2). We know there is a Lord over this land we are in, even while we choose to ignore His laws.

Mankind in rebellion against that God will foolishly declare the physical world to be purposeless plastic, to be given purpose only by their own will. They declare that they are their own gods and go about to use the physical world as they choose to do. They are like that spoiled kid vandalizing cars in a foreign land, thinking their status makes them immune to the caning. What is moral is what they choose to do. If they choose sexually to do this or that thing, who is to say they are wrong? This foolish reasoning leads to chaos and destruction. Can we imagine a moral world where hands can be used to labor or kill, and both were equally commendable moral acts? But this is exactly what we do with the sexual members of our body. That is the end of egalitarian philosophy. Applying this moral philosophy to sexual actions is no less horrific. How far down the road of moral depravity is one willing to permit the culture to drift toward before they are willing to recognize true distinctions? Arbitrary lines in the sand, such as illusive definitions of words like consent, are easily erased by shifting winds of depraved rationality. Anything can be justified by autonomous mankind. That means absolutely anything. As Dostoevsky argued, if there is no God then all things are permissible, or now, even commendable.

So, how did God intend for us to use this world? Do we use it according to His design or contrary to it (Rom 1:26, 27)? The answer here is obvious. One can use or misuse this world (I Cor 7:31). Set aside for a moment the idea that God has indeed spoken and has given expressed commands that should govern our lives (see Antithesis # 3). He is there and He is not silent, as Schaffer had proclaimed. But focus right now on the fact that He is indeed there and what is has its being according to His will in its creation and sustaining. That is the true ethic, whether in relation to God as He is known in or by the things He made or in the Scriptures. God takes pleasure in His will and by necessity takes no pleasure in any who would resist it. He is Lord over all that is and over all that I should do, even my sexuality. How I use my body and its members is something that is to be ordered by the Lord and is to be submitted to His evaluation. That is, if you wish to be right with God and on the right side of His will.

James captured this aspect of ethics in regard to the totality of how we live and behave in this life. If we know to do good and we do not do it, it is sin (James 4:17). What James intended to say is that the known good, which if we fail to do is evil, is the seeking of God's will in all things we do (full context, James 4:13–17). This idea is far more profound than many ignorant and legalistic ministers have portrayed it. Exhausted parishioners have fainted under the load of good things their ministers have told them they should be doing. James marks the difference between two separate ways that people prosecute their lives. James introduced this absolute ethical imperative with the word, "Therefore . . . ." It was, contextually, the conclusion of the argument that he had been making in the previous verses. What is evil is described by reference to the people who think that their will determines their own life (James 4:13). This is secularism, living or acting as if there was no God, regardless of whether one nominally confesses that God is. They say to themselves that, by their own will, they will continue to live and do this thing or that. They do this without any thought of God (Ps 10). They have not retained God in their knowledge or rather they set themselves as final arbiters of their schemes and judged that God was unnecessary to their prosecution (Rom 1:28). So, they go about living their lives, doing what is right in their own eyes (Deut 12:8). But what is truly good is that which is first predicated on the will of God (James 4:15). All people are ethically bound, they ought to confess, according to James, that their life and all that they do is predicated on what the Lord wills. This is what it means to believe in His Lordship or Sovereignty, God has the right to command our lives. We may do that which is admired by others in this world and at the same time be doing that which is profoundly and fundamentally evil, if how we live and what we do is not built on what the will of God is. The rich fool learned this very thing in the end (Luke 12:16–21).

Too few in this life think like this on a fundamental level, even those who profess Christ as Lord. If I am to be an ethical person, I must seek to know and then act on what I believe the will of the Lord is. This is what separates the sinful autonomous person from the faithful ethical person, full dependency on the Lord as Lord to direct their life.

What does knowledge of the Creator/creature distinction teach me about how I am supposed to live? It teaches me that there is a purpose created in things that is not decided, ordered, or evaluated by me. Life is neither subjective nor nihilistic. These things, including the very members of my body, are ordered by God. The very members of my body have teleological purposes given by God alone. I must bow before the Lord in these things. I must use nature without abusing it (I Cor 7:31). I must treat people as if they are created in the image of God. I must treat my body as it is in all reality, something given purpose by its Creator. There is a real and true ethic to the use of my body, and it is intended to show that my body has its Lord. Therefore, my hands ought to labor, to give instead of steal, they ought to care and not kill, my mouth ought to bless and not curse, and so on. This is no less true when contemplating the sexual members of our bodies.

Paul drew this same conclusion about the body. What James corrected in secular philosophy; Paul corrected in hedonistic philosophy. We cannot continue in a self-contained cycle, believing that our appetites exist solely to be pleased by the things that are there to satisfy them, and those things simply exist solely to satisfy our autonomous appetites. He said that hedonistic philosophy could be boiled down to this maxim, "belly for the meat and meat for the belly" (I Cor 6:13). This was Paul's argument against a life lived in sexual immorality, and it is summed up with this indicative, "the body is not for fornication" (I Cor 6:13). What did Paul conclude was the way that we should live? He said in that same text that "the body is for the Lord and the Lord is for the body." In other words, as James had taught, the body is meant to seek the will of God and to be pleased in the Lord's will. We are no happier than when living in His will. There is no greater delight than walking according to the law of God (Ps 1).

This idea of Lordship, therefore, is applied even to our sexual choices. This being so, we should seek the will of God in all that entails that realm. We must ask, what intent did God have for creating sex? God's chief design for sex is, though not its only obvious purpose, for procreation.[4] Rebellion against nature attempts to divorce this purpose from sex through the prevention of life. It also attempts to divorce sex from life by asserting and normalizing relationships that deny or defy life in principle or type. But sex is meant to continue life, to be life giving. This is why God chiefly gave it as Lord of creation, a creation abounding and perpetuating life. "Let each bring forth after their kind" (Gen 1:24, 25). Without sex life would not continue.

Procreation would entail not just the act that potentially brings new life into the world. It would involve the care and commitment toward the relational context within which that life is created (respect and dignity of the woman by the man, and vice versa). It would involve the purposive care and nurture of new life created. All this having God as its final cause, the direction and pursuit for which procreation occurs. The Psalmist brought this out by declaring the imperative of the generations to communicate faith to other generations, that the generation to come might know God, fear God, know and keep His commandments (His will), and hope in Him (Ps. 78:1–8). Such imperatives are rooted in the Law of Moses (Deut 6:4–9). The idea of an absent or detached fatherhood or motherhood is alien to scriptural sexual ethics. The moral obligation of the Lordship of God in the matter of sexuality extends much further than the morality of the sexual act itself, the act cannot be detached morally from God's purposes. It extends to all that may come from the act. It extends to the idea of being a faithful husband and wife, and nurturing parents for the glory of God. Sex outside of the life-giving and life-sustaining purposes of

4. Although, it is important to note, as created by God, purposes beyond procreation complement and do not contradict its chief purpose.

God is rebellion against the Sovereign. They are trading in counterfeit currency and not the true.

The act itself, though, may transgress the bounds of God's design as well. Sexual acts may go outside of God's set physical design. They may transgress God's moral boundaries. This is something any honest sexual ethic must hold. The practice of our current culture of entering into the act without real commitment to the other person, using the other instead for pleasure to be discarded afterward, like the rind of a piece of fruit, is an example of such a transgression. While the law is not specifically before us at this point in our conversation, the law laid guilt on certain acts and called some an abomination to God, something that displeases or is offensive to Him.

The point here, then, is that sex is a creation that stands in the presence of God to be evaluated. This is the point of discomfort for those who reject God. God is pleased when the creature acts according to His will alone and displeased when it is not so. So, every sexual decision that we make, either to ponder on it in the privacy of our own minds or act out on it in public or private, is a moral decision that is either good or evil before our God. It either conforms to God as Lord or rejects Him as Lord. It is moral because it counts (i.e., is accountable) and it matters. It is moral because it happens before the Lord that has established moral reality and will judge all moral choices, either in this life or in the life to come. All sexual immorality, like the existence of evil itself, is a deviation from the good that God brought into being. As the Lord over sexuality, God has greater ends than secularism and hedonism can proclaim (who either deny that it has an end or make the end some selfish and self-interested thing). To proclaim those greater ends and point away from sexual sins is not to kill imagined fun but to lead us to the Lord and His greater ends.

Anthropology and Sex
Antitheses 2: The Male and the Female

*"So God created man in his own image, in the image of God
created he him; male and female created he them." Genesis 1:27*

Now, SETTING ASIDE THE morality fixed in the Creator/creation
distinction, what does nature and even the nature of God teach
us about sexuality? It would be helpful at this point to step back
and consider Egalitarian arguments from the Scriptures regarding
sexuality as it relates to the nature of God and the nature of the
things that have been created by God. It is certainly not counterin-
tuitive to point out that human sexuality is built on the fundamental principle that each human being has a sex or gender. It would
be irrational to discuss sexuality otherwise. In order to have sex,
according to the most basic definition of the word, implies that
each participant is a sexual being. One engages in sex because one
is sexual in nature and possesses in their person definite sexual
attributes.[1] These attributes are real and are defined and dispensed
to each person by God. Therefore, they carry authority. Nature
is the authority of God in creating all its contingencies. The term
gender (as opposed to the term sex) describes the language that
we use to describe what God has wrought in reality. This language
ought itself to reflect God as Lord and not to deny Him. Only in a
culture that has embraced the most extreme egalitarian views can

---

1. This is not in the Freudian sense that all that drives us is sexual.

this even be questioned, which is an indictment on our culture, our churches, and the egalitarian philosophy at large today.

Anthropology is the study of man, as man relates to the rest of the created order. The biblical creation view allows for individuals to exist with real distinct sexual functions. It proceeds from Logos and not Chaos. This immediately runs contrary to the politics of the Left embedded in the language of the elite. They envision something like Huxley's *Brave New World* where all are equal (without distinctions), all babies are engineered outside of the sexual process, all sex is just for play, and all life from beginning to end is controlled by a centralized human authority. The life-giving relationship of the family is a political enemy of such a view but will prevail as it represents the Lordship of the one true God. There is a symbiosis to sexual reality, or as Paul said, the woman is not without the man and the man is not without the woman (I Cor. 11:11). More on this later. These are distinctions created by God and they exist and thrive on the concrete reality of one another. He created humanity with sexuality, male and female (Gen. 1:27).

There are two classes of arguments that are made to support egalitarianism when answering against Christian assertions of the created order. There is the argument from anthropology (the nature of the human being) and the argument from anthropomorphic descriptions of God (deriving propositions about anthropology from the nature of God). Each of these deserves a short commentary as we nail down an understanding of human sexuality.

Consider the egalitarian arguments from the anthropology of the Scriptures. Overall, the view of anthropology has been skewed by the advent of scientific materialism and science fiction. If there is no supernatural God and all things can be explained by material processes alone, or worse, purposeless random events, then all that is simply is what it is. Whatever that happens to be. There is no morality in such a scheme for whatever happens is natural, whether that be charity or holocaust. There is no set nature of anything in such a philosophical view, a way we ought to be. It all develops in flux. What it is today is not what it was yesterday or what it will be tomorrow. All is changing according to laws of cause and effect (a universal they cannot account for in their worldview). There is no truth or morality or beauty in such a world. There is no way to know a changing thing to be anything specifically. There is no way to even know that we know anything at all, since our mind itself is nothing more than the product of cause and effect, a constantly changing thing. If scientific materialism can offer any answers at all, it would only be incoherent gibberish asserting nothing. But such is the state of current scientific ideology. It serves egalitarianism well but says nothing meaningful. It speaks with authority to ultimately say that nothing can be said with any authority. It usually sounds smart, so the masses believe it. The worst thing you can be called currently is a science denier.

Science fiction comes along in that same vein and offers us a different view of anthropology and sexuality. With an empty promise of endless technological progress, everyone will one day be able to make and remake themselves according to their own will. And it assumes that such progress is part of the history of the universe and to speak against it in any way is to be on "the wrong side of history." What has developed by chance here through the law of cause and effect, as we reach out into the vast universe, there must be many different ways that life has developed. This is the Star Trek view of the universe. There could be, if we explored, many different expressions of sexuality and gender among "sentient" beings. Therefore, the authority of science fiction convinces us that we must not have any dogmatic view of sexuality and gender here and now. Therefore, they say, all the possible contingencies leave it open for the individual to express free choice in creating their own sexual expression. Contingencies in nature, however, are expressions of the free will of God as Lord and not the free will of mankind. We can only subdue what God put under our power, not change the nature of anything He made. To base what you believe on what cannot possibly be observed is a fiction indeed. And to deny human nature because other natures exist in theory or in observation is nothing more than rebellion against His Lordship and His created order.

The fact is this, what we have is the world that God has created, which we can see and observe and the nature He freely chose to give to us. God created man and woman, as they are. While God created the Seahorse a certain way, sexually speaking, we can observe that God has created mankind a certain way, sexually speaking. Mankind is not dogkind and to conflate them is to assert an ugly moral monster out of mankind. God speaks of human sexuality in the Scriptures repeatedly and without contradiction. The male produces seed. The female is impregnated by the seed of the male. The female carries, births, and nurtures the child produced. In the ethics of the Scripture, there is a process in which the man raised in such a reality will also take a wife and be faithful to her. Children ought to be brought forth in this continuing reality. Codified in the law, the children obey and honor both their parents, mother and father (Gen 2:23, 24, Ex 20:12). Marriage and parentage that sees sexual distinctions and even systems of leadership are the uniform declaration of Scriptures. Or, in other words, human sexuality can be defined as such; man and woman, becoming husband and wife, becoming father and mother, producing men and women who follow the same process for the glory of God.

Anthropology is not independent of the Lord. The fear of the Lord is the starting point for all knowledge (Prov. 1:7). That would include any knowledge about the human being that is fearfully and wonderfully made by God (Ps. 139). The purpose of sexuality in nature, as given by the God, is for the continuance of human life and for the blessings of prosperity to the same. "And God blessed them, and God said unto them, Be fruitful, and multiply, and replenish the earth, and subdue it: and have dominion over the fish of the sea, and over the fowl of the air, and over every living thing that moveth upon the earth" (Gen 1:28). It is for the good of humanity, not just in any one individual life but across generations, a means of life continuing in the knowledge and blessings of God. The promise to Abraham was across generations (Gen. 12:1–3). Any arbitrary and relative purpose divorced from the teleological end of God in sexuality falls far short of the grand blessedness found in the nature of human sexuality. To say sex is for momentary pleasure, or for individual human identity, or for self-fulfillment of one isolated being may seem grand but leaves one empty in the end. None of the advertisements or philosophies regarding sex have anything to do with the broader purpose of life given by God. After 6,000 to 10,000 years of human history, humanity is still here because of sex and the distinctions the Lord made. The knowledge of God is still propagated from generation to generation because the Lord gave us distinctions or rather antithesis.

I recently saw an advertisement for pregnancy tests which showed three women taking the test and the first two of them were hoping that it was negative due to it not fitting into their plans. From the killing of children in the womb, to the free love and casual sex movement of the Sexual Revolution, to policies that break down the normative purpose of the nuclear family, modern sexual ethics is opposed to the life giving and human thriving purposes of God. Empty scientific and materialistic philosophies under-girded by bad eschatology found in science fiction is deprived of any grander purpose for human sexuality above the fleeting moment of the individual experiencing pleasure or having relative validation in their own self-contained life. It remains to be seen the destructive influence that ideology will have on culture as it merits the judgment of its Lord.

The bottom line theologically regarding sex and anthropology is that it is created by God for grander ends than a momentary act of pleasure or a self-contained expression of individuality. The first command was to be fruitful and multiply and fill the earth (Gen 1:28). The perspective is generational and bigger than any individual life or isolated act. And it has knowing and glorifying God as its broader goal (Ps 78:1–8). The act of sex is connected with generational work of people knowing God and hoping in Him. Any holistic view of sexuality that does not have this broad inter-generational, God-centered, aspect of anthropology fails to truly understand human sexuality. God given human sexuality has general human flourishing at its core. The Biblical narrative is filled with genealogies. The bringing of Christ into the world is brought to us via a "this person begat this person" phraseology.

The Christian sexual ethic includes bringing up children in the nurture and teaching of the Lord (Eph 6:4). It has a greater nature than ideas of individual self-expression or endless meaningless cycles of pleasure seeking can ever teach. People who have a sex (given by God) have sex (as an activity created by God) as part of a far greater historical purpose (the good and flourishing of humanity throughout the whole of history). Sexuality is not an incidental or periphery fact asserted into Scriptures but related to the whole of our faith as lived out in real history. Christians have children believing God has ongoing purposes for those children in space and time. We cannot deny its purposes and ends without eventually denying and distorting the whole of the Scriptures.

Following the progression of Christ, we see what we have already asserted. God created *male and female*, they become one together in marriage as *husband and wife*, being husband and wife, they become *mother and father*, and from there they produce children (male and female) who grow to start the process again. These are the repeated terms of sexuality as a doctrine prevalent in what God has spoken in the Scriptures. Thus, sexuality as created by its Lord is for the continuance of physical human life and its godly thriving (Matt 19:4–6). The Lord is its first cause. The Lord is the final cause. In the progression dictated by Christ is the mechanism by which each generation may know and glorify its God. There is a generational purpose and good in sexuality and a great amount of evil and death in its negation. For, if sexuality is perverted, it diminishes the physical life and health of the race of man and it brings up the horrible possibility of a generation of men being raised up that know not God and wish not to give Him glory. All of this is predicated on these simple truths, our Lord created and is Lord over human sexuality and all distinctions that He made are real and holy. To deny those distinctions is to deny God as Lord.

So, egalitarianism is a denial of Lordship and divinely given distinctions. How then can one argue from Scriptural anthropology any form of egalitarianism in the nature of human sexuality? Other than reading the Scripture through the lens of scientific materialism and science fiction, there remains a misunderstanding or wresting of two elements of anthropology that are used to imply egalitarianism.

There is the truth that male and female (even though distinct from each other in terms of sexuality) are yet *equally* created in the image of God (Gen 1:27). Is there not egalitarian equality taught here? It is implied by some that it is only ignorance in the authors of the Scriptures, and/or those interpreting them, to believe that the outworking of sexuality has distinctions. It is asserted that there can be no system of leadership in which the husband and father are in a position of authority and the wife is in any way in a position of support. If someone like Paul makes such declarations, then they are simply wrong or just a reflection of an outmoded primitive culture (I Tim 2:11–14, Eph. 5:22–24). Since such language is inherent to Scriptures in the realm of church polity and in the home, ultimately to hold to egalitarianism means that one must abandon the idea that Scriptures speak authoritatively and consistently in its totality. Thus, the egalitarian will ultimately freely ignore passages of Scripture that contradict their assertions as being irrelevant.

It should be admitted here that there are abuses among sinful men in the outworking of ideas of leadership and support, a misappropriation of that which is declared by the Scriptures. Just as Scriptures have been wrongly used to defend chattel slavery, so sinful men use it wrongly to justify domestic violence, controlling behavior, and other sins. Just because these abuses have occurred does not mean that the distinctions declared by the Scriptures are wrong. God most definitely has created differences between male and female and has in those distinctions given definite roles to each in the outworking of sexuality in this world. To one it is given to be a female, a wife, and a mother. To the other it is given to be a male, a husband, and a father.

Ultimately, without getting into the minutia of particular texts, there are greater truths of God that we learn from those distinctions. We learn what a true loving Father is from God's relationship with the world (as His offspring) and with the believer that has been adopted through salvation into His family. Fatherhood is good as we learn it from God and not from its bad examples among men. We also learn the love and sacrifice of a husband in what Christ accomplished in the gospel. We learn the wonderful nature of the submission of the church to its husband, Christ. Submission to a good husband (Christ) who loves and gives Himself for His wife (the church) is revealed to us in the outworking of sexual distinctions that God has ordered and made in the real world. But that is something that will be explored further as we proceed.

So, what does male and female being equally created in the image of God mean? It means that they are equal in value and worth and dignity. They both equally have that which is like God imparted to them (intellect, will, emotions, a spiritual nature). They are equally made to know and enjoy God, the substance of what they are but shadows. Just as one man cannot kill another because they are created in the image of God (Gen 9:6), so neither man nor woman can be sinned against without a demand of justice. Both are equal before our eyes, neither can be justly defrauded or injured without those that do so being guilty before God. God's image in both is apparent and not to be maligned by sinning against either. The equal worth of each male and female created in the image of God is not diminished in the order God gave, any more than God making the Aaronic line of high priests made them superhuman or those whom they served in that office less than human. These distinctions become important as God reveals truth to us. If man was autonomous then man being head over the woman would be abusive and demeaning. But, since the head of every man is Christ then the role of the man is submitted to the Lord just as much as the role of the woman to the husband (I Cor. 11:3).

The institution of sexuality is from the beginning (i.e., the process of male/female becoming husband/wife becoming father/mother and so on, Matt. 19:3–9). It is the first expression of human government before God, outside of the individual conscience, and intended by God to be the reality from which human society continues generation after generation. It preceded the formal law and the gospel and all forms of human government as the foundation of all human relationships. Its fundamental structure is essential to humanity and nothing within its structure is a detriment to the worth of any individual, male or female. Rather, it establishes their most fundamental purposes in this life.[2]

The current philosophy of sexuality has not yielded a deep sense of purpose. Individual autonomy produces listlessness. If you do not know where you are supposed to go, you should not be surprised when you end up nowhere. A deeper sense of true patriarchy where the head of every man is the Lord is a better way than egalitarianism. It is better because it is given by an all wise God. True patriarchy creates men who faithfully love and minister to their wives. They cleave to them. It fosters a real and true matriarchy where the children continue under the nurturing authority of both parents till they faithfully cleave to their own family. Patriarchal leadership under the rule of the Lord, supported by a godly matriarchy, creates a stable structure for families and culture. To be equally created in the image of God is about equal dignity and not a negation of our Lord and His distinctions.

A further argument from anthropology is in regards to the gospel. It is argued that Paul asserted the principles of egalitarianism by saying that in Christ there is neither male nor female. Paul said, "For as many of you as have been baptized into Christ have put on Christ. There is neither Jew nor Greek, there is neither bond nor free, there is neither male nor female: for ye are all one in Christ Jesus. And if ye be Christ's, then are ye Abraham's seed, and heirs according to the promise" (Gal 3:27–29). However, Paul and the Holy Spirit who moved him to write would not be contradicting what was taught about distinctions and differing roles (I Tim 2:11–14). It is disingenuous to claim Paul as an authority only when he says something that seems to agree with my position. However, Paul is not asserting ontological egalitarianism here. To assert that each are loved by Christ equally, equally heirs of salvation and fellow helpers in its propagation, and equally representative of Christ in their confession does not contradict an

---

2. Unless God has gifted or called one to singleness or providentially hindered them from seeking such purposes for His own greater reasons or for the sake of the kingdom of God, Matt 19:12, I Cor 7:7.

assertion of distinction in roles. That we are brothers and sisters, equally loved by the one that saved us, is not to say we do not have differing purposes given to us by God, as Lord, in this life. God can make distinctions without disturbing salvific equality in His grace (I Cor 12:4–6).

There is a profound truth of equality found in salvation. In Christ, that is in the same profession of faith in Him, there is no division of class, ethnicity, or gender. We all equally have put on Christ by the outward confession of baptism. We all have equally entered into the inheritance of the seed of Abraham. We are all equally free from the condemnation of the law and saved in Christ. Some take this declaration that in Christ there is neither male nor female to mean that egalitarianism may now be applied to all things. The inference is that these necessarily must dissipate. But, they cannot exegete from the text itself to apply beyond what we all have in Christ and His salvation, especially when it comes to distinctions inherent in sexuality.

When we enter the home (that which relates immediately to sexuality) or the church (that which relates allegorically to sexuality), we enter that which is governed by the Lord. If He as Lord has spoken in any way about the roles that each of His servants play in those realms, then His rule is to be upheld. This would not destroy the equality of salvation to uphold the distinctions of roles played by those who serve Him as Lord.

And so, we have seen scriptural anthropology in a nutshell. There is a place for true equality and godly distinctions in sexuality. The blurring of all distinctions is not honoring to the rule of God. But, there is yet one more line of scriptural arguments touted by egalitarian proponents.

Egalitarianism will also argue from the nature of God and assert propositions about humanity from God's nature. This involves the anthropomorphic revelation of God. That being this, how God revealed Himself to mankind in common terms understood by mankind. This will touch on secular critical theories, like Queer Theory, and its contemporary influence as a lens through which theology is read, especially when it comes to gendered truths declared by the Scriptures. The basis of these secular theories is the assumption of egalitarianism, that all gendered truths are nothing more than social constructs without reality.

Egalitarianism not only attempts to declare that God is not distinct from creation, but it will also deny any reality to God making distinct claims in the revelation of Himself. I have already offended the egalitarian sensibility by speaking of God with gendered distinction, "Himself." That offends in its distinction of God as God, and not the same as all else, and it offends in its gendering. Why would I speak of God with gendered terminology? Does God have a gender and if so, or if not, what does it teach us about human sexuality?

It is important to note that morality and moral choices happen in the context of moral law, that is related to how things are in the context in which the Lord created them outside of and distinct from Himself. We could just say that God is ontologically different than man and close this conversation without further comment. Showing us that God is not like His creation does not free us from moral obligations laid upon us within the boundaries He has made in His creation. Therefore, the line of thought that says that God is a Spirit (which is a true scriptural declaration, John 4:24), and therefore is neither male nor female, and this means that we also have or should have no sexual distinctions is foolish. This is an improper use of an *a fortiori* argument.

It is true that God indeed is a Spirit and not a physical or material reality. God is not sexual. It does not however follow that this sweeps away sexual distinctions. Those distinctions flow from Him being God and all else that is not Him not being God (the creature/Creator distinction). God created the distinctions of sexuality and in those distinctions, He is Lord over us. Again, the morality of sexuality comes from Him being Lord over what He has created. Sexual morality is not based on the ontology of God as God, but it is based on the Lordship of God as He has revealed truth (epistemologically) in the purpose (teleologically) of the things He made (ontologically). In other words, our moral obligations rise no higher than what God has made known to us regarding the nature and purposes of the things He created. God does not have hands, but He made us to have hands and our hands to have purpose based on His revelation to us. Thus, we work with our hands and give instead of killing. We do not say that since God does not have hands that we do not have hands or that our hands have no moral purposes. This is true of sexuality as well. God being different from us does not leave us knowing nothing of His will in the matter of sexuality.

I heard one Christian philosopher say that we all have a sex because God has a sex. That is somewhat of a misleading statement. God is not sexual in the sense that we are. The false god of Mormonism is a sexual god that performs actual sexual acts to bring forth children, much like the former pagan deities. The true God, however, is life and life-giving. Therefore, by analogy, we speak of concepts like procreation. But He does not have a physical body and is not sexual. That is a creature distinction. God is a Spirit (John 4:24). Therefore, we do not make images of God and worship them as if they were Him (Deut. 4:15–20). A physical God, absent incarnational truth, is not the God of the Bible. The limited and depraved gods of paganism are sexual and often even immorally so. Those false deities are gods made into the image of mankind, idols. The one true God is not like these. God is personal[3] and therefore speaks of Himself as personal. God speaks with personal pronouns. And God, and those He revealed Himself to (the writers of the Scriptures), used gendered pronouns (e.g., He) and gendered nouns (e.g., Father, Son, King) to speak of Himself. This is not because gendered language truly described a biological truth about the ontology of God, but is, as I will shortly speak and is the chief thesis of this short line of thought, a revelation of theological truth. In the same way, we speak of God as having hands (to speak of His ability), as having arms (to speak of His power), and as having eyes and ears (to speak of His knowledge). He does not actually have these physical features any more than He has wings, feathers, is a burning furnace, or a loaf of bread (all

---

3. Or, better yet, He is super-personal, containing in Himself community as well as unity in the Trinity.

pictures used of God in the Scriptures). These are analogical truths of God. He does have knowledge, power, and so on. This is what is called anthropomorphisms, God speaking of Himself in human terms. However, this becomes a point of controversy for those who hold egalitarian views.

Procreation is an imperfect picture of the one that is and has life in Himself, the one that gives to all life and being. Gendered language is meant to be used to speak truly of reality, not what may be or what one wishes to be. Yet, God is exclusively described (even by Himself) with masculine gendered nouns and pronouns. The leap is then made that if God is not biologically sexual then the gendered language is either meaningless at best or relics of mistaken patriarchy at worse. Then a further leap is made to say that we should abolish all gendered language of God and of the things God has created. The assumed truth is that all such language of God is without significance and meaning. This erring judgment then is applied to the things (with definite distinctions) that God has made. Without warrant they say the things that God made have no real distinctions and are therefore without moral obligations.

Where then does gender or sexuality come from? Is it a reality in God? Is it that God has a sex? God is eternal and does not need to do anything to continue on. He is that He is. He has neither come to be as being produced by something else nor is there any that will come after God in the sense of becoming. "Before me there was no God formed, neither shall there be after me" (Isa 43:10). In that sense, God is not sexual and is neither the product of generational activity nor is He producing further generations of Gods after Him. God simply is. The pagan gods were described as being produced by generations before and themselves producing gods after them. The same is true of other polytheistic schemes.

However, gendered truths find their ground in God. God has eternally begotten His Son and brought Him forth. When we look at the eternal reality of God, as God has made it known to us, we see the love of a Father who has His Son in His bosom (John 1:18). He has made Himself known in a familial context, distinct persons eternally in reciprocal relation to one another. There is love and nurture in God.

So, God is not physical. He does not procreate sexually. He is different from His creation. But God is the ground of the concept of bringing forth and nurturing, which is the ideal of the created sexual order of the creature. We are in the process of generation. God is not in that process but is the ontological ground of it. We came through the sexual order created by God. We produce further generations. We once were not and those that will come from us are not yet. And what happens in that sexual order speaks of the truths of God.

God has brought outside of Himself all physical reality. We are all, in this sense, the offspring of God (Acts 17:28). God as Lord of all creation begats (as with Adam specifically, Luke 3:38) and cares for and nurtures and disciplines (Heb. 12:5–11). All that we would understand as necessary and good gendered ideas both of men and women can find their reference points in the goodness of God. This is especially true when it comes to God's covenant with His people, those whom He had chosen to be their Lord. He nourished Israel as a nursing mother (Deut 2:18, Isa 42:14, 66:13). He longed to protect them as a hen brings her chicks under her wing (Ps 91:4, Matt 23:37). He relates to the saved as a Father and gives to them as to His children (Matt 7:11). There are even greater truths than these. God is neither male or female but is the ground of all that is good in each and each may find their reference point, even in the sexual order, by the image of God in which they were created. What makes a female a female is not societal structures or expectations (reasonable or unreasonable), but rather the image of God. God creates. When a man and woman engage in sex together, they are engaging in a potential act of procreation in cooperation with God. It is an enlivening and potential life-giving act that teaches something of the joy and life-giving acts of God.

God created the female as female to exhibit His glory in a specific way. It has nothing to do with makeup, fashion, mannerisms, activities, or societal expectations. God created the male as male to exhibit His glory in a different way. It is in this that He decided to reveal specific truths of Himself, and especially the truths of the gospel. In the creation account, the male is created differently sexually, and it becomes the type of what God Himself would do in salvation. We see the truth in Christ. He left His abiding (as represented by the man leaving His father and mother) in order to cleave to His bride in marriage (rescuing a people for Himself) to be one with them (bone of their bone, one flesh). Christ with His bride is a theological truth that is brought to bear in the terms of sexuality. We understand the gospel and the love of God toward mankind by the things that God has created. The fulness of this will be discussed later.

Egalitarianism causes us to lose the distinctions that make understanding gospel truths possible. They declare that sexual distinctions are only an illusion or false construct. Sex or gender is not something that we are but only something, by our own acts of will, we decide to be and then express. While it is true that we do express sexual truths, a woman will do things that assert their perceptions of femininity and so will a man.[4] But it is in reference to what they truly are as created by God.

So why call God by gendered terms? God has made Himself known in masculine terms, even though we know that God is a Spirit and not flesh. He is gendered even though we know that God is the basis for all true virtues related to sexuality, male and female, and their image is springing from Him. Can we consider the masculine terms of God as superfluous or without significance? Are we free to refer to God in feminine pronouns (she or her) or with feminine titles (mother, goddess)? Do we further infer from the ontology of God that there is no ontological truth to our sexuality? The latter is an absurdity. We are not God and our reality is determined by God. We are what we are ontologically and teleologically by the Sovereignty of the Lord, as an expression of His will. To the former questions the answer is emphatic, no we are not free

---

4. These, admittedly, may in a fallen world be distorted perceptions of femininity and masculinity not based on the revealed truths of God - "He must be a female because he is emotional." Or, "she must be a male because she is assertive or enjoys sports."

to define God as we choose, any more than we are free to define ourselves as we choose. He is Lord. God alone is free to define Himself. His freedom to define Himself can in no way infer a right for us to define ourselves contrary to Him. That would be like us saying we are Lord and not Him. When He speaks in the matter of self-revelation, He declares the truth and reality about Himself.

There is significant meaning to the terms He uses, and those terms establish not just ontological truth, but theological truth. Sexual truths speak to us about how God has decided to relate to us, His creatures. There is truth in what He has revealed. We cannot change the language and terms of that truth without changing what He has meant to say. We do not create truth, He does. We cannot change the truths of sexuality, as He created them, without doing damage to theological truth. The unspoken truth is that this is why there is a connection between egalitarian ideas of the sexual revolution and the deconstruction movement that leads many in denouncing their faith in Christ. We are not, as the lie of the serpent says, gods. We do not determine moral truth, He alone does. We can speak rightly and practice rightly in the realm of sexuality if we are submitted to Him and His will.

The truths of sexuality are determined by God through what He has created and what He has revealed about Himself through analogy. When we bring an authority independent of God into the realm of sexuality, we have challenged the authority of the one ruling that realm. We cannot plant the flag of our own authority or some other arbitrary authority and claim that the realm is not His. We must contend with Him there. He drew the boundaries. His laws alone rule there. We are rebels if we begin to assert our authority contrary to His. We are deceivers if we begin to try to arrange the boundaries to fit our will. He owns the Land. He sets the boundaries. He is Lord, even here in terms of our sexuality! And any anthropology that defines man outside of the context of God as Lord over him, and outside of the context of the created order God placed him in, can speak no truth concerning man.

The Morality of Sex
Antithesis 3: That Which is Good and That Which is Evil

"The body is not for fornication but for the Lord." First Corinthians 6:13

IF THE HUMAN BODY has ontological purpose given to it by the Lord, then it has a definite moral context in which it exists. Nothing we do in the body is a morally neutral act. The Creator/creature distinction gives the only true ground for morality. Dostoevsky would say that without God all things are permissible, but with God there are distinctions that are evaluated by His judgment. He gives and reveals His purposes as Lord.

This moves naturally into the realm of religion, without which any discussion of the categories of right and wrong, good and evil, are rendered meaningless. We cannot hold to a perennial philosophy as touted by Huxley or Jung in our ontology, that all is one and all religions are expressions of the same oneness. This oneness, or egalitarianism, now being applied to religious truth, erases all distinctions and therefore all moral obligations in religious thought. Picture all possible religious beliefs as being branches springing from one tree and therefore all equally true manifestations of the nature of the tree. That is the perennial philosophy of religion. Without any ontological distinctions, all moral distinctions in belief and practice are now abolished as well. This opens the door to the embracing of logical contradiction in faith. But God cannot be and not be, be personal and non personal, non-judgmental and the judge of all things, etc. This foolish philosophy that denies the distinction of creature and Creator cannot say anything is true and therefore cannot say anything is good.

The moral implications of it are outrageous. We know that loving sexual acts in marriage are morally different than gang rape or child rape (forgive the extremeness of these parallels). There is not a perennial connection or oneness in those things, they are not equally good expressions. One is evil and one is good. One worships the Creator and the other is to be judged. One is a fool to hold perennial philosophy regarding sexual morality, just as one is a fool to believe it about God. In the same way, one is a fool to hold that the Lord is not distinct from everything else. There is a Lord that is judging all moral desires and outcomes as either good or evil.

There is no controversy for the believer when it is said that the law of God is holy and good (Rom 7:12). The Psalmist summed up the attitude of one in a right relationship with God by saying that he delighted to do the will of God (Ps 40:8). When one desires to please God, the commandments of God are not grievous things (I John 5:3). They are expressions of a longing in the heart to honor their Lord. Every commandment is an opportunity of worship. If we are cognizant of the will of God for us to obey the laws of the magistrate, then obeying traffic laws becomes a means of us declaring the absolute Lordship of God over us. We may even find ourselves joyous in that realm because of this truth. How much more when we discover the will of God as expressed in commandments for the use of our bodies? God, who is worthy of all worship, has spoken and made His will known. God, who is over all, has spoken and revealed His will in nature and in history.

That does not mean that understanding the nature and scope of any of the commands of God is necessarily grasped by all who profess to believe. There are some commands that will leave us bewildered. Specific commands were given at specific times by the Lord to certain people. We, being alienated from the full context, have a difficult time comprehending these. When God commanded

THE MORALITY OF SEX

Abram to offer Isaac, it was also bewildering to Abram for sure (Gen 22:2). But that command was Abram's and not ours, even though it is meaningful to us in many ways. Why would God command that the Israelite not sow their fields with mixed types of seeds or not to wear linen and wool mixed (Deut 22:9, 11)? And does it mean that we are sinning if we are doing those things? And, if we could come up with a satisfactory answer, such as, He is Lord and He desired them to appear in all ways to be separated unto Him, how would we know whether such commands are directly relevant to us now? How would we even measure our compliance in a culture so far removed from that original context? We can easily say that when God judged other nations it was not because they failed to obey such ambiguous laws (See Lev 18).

The believer, who has already grasped the truth that God is Lord over all His creatures, has no problem thinking in terms of right and wrong, good and evil. Just the bare possession of those categories does not do away with all ambiguities and honest questions. We cannot allow the unbeliever to mock such commands as if they were silly. God is not mocked. He has a right to order all parts of our life; how we dress, how we eat, how we work. He had that authority then and He still has that same authority now. Whatever the context and meaning of those ambiguities may have been then, in principle they still are to be obeyed by all who are true worshippers of God now. It is only the one that rejects God that contends with obvious and clear commands by saying that they do not understand the ambiguous ones. My ability to understand the command not to wear mixed threads has never caused me to say that adultery and murder must then be acceptable and good now. That is an absurdity.

The controversy arises when those less clear and ambiguous commands are carried beyond the threshold of personal opinion, at least in this present evil world, if not even among the fellowship of believers. Legalism in its most benign form says that those ambiguities are important for all believers to strictly keep. If one wishes to go to church on a certain day of the week and is convinced in their own conscience that such a thing is right for them to do, and does so with likeminded people, they are rightly living out their faith in being convinced in their own mind (Rom 14:5). There is no clear command that says the Christian must worship at such and such a place and time and all arguments are in the realm of ambiguity. If that person will say that all who do not practice as they do are sinning, then they have crossed over into the realm of legalism. One can wear mixed clothes or not wear mixed clothes today, depending on their conviction about what the law actually teaches or means in its original context and how it is applied presently (all necessary and often complicated steps in biblical hermeneutics, especially in murky matters such as these). But they cannot demand their neighbors comply or judge them for coming to differing convictions about what pleases their Lord (Rom 14:1–6). This is not approaching such a subject in the spirit of Christian charity. Worse yet, in the most malignant form of legalism, they may go about to declare that all who do not practice as they do are lost and without Christ, or even go about to persecute those who do not do as they do. This becomes sin to them and may even become the declaration of another gospel (Gal 1:6, 7).

Is this what the Christian is doing with the subject of sexuality? That is the claim of the sexually perverse. Are we, when we declare sexual morality from the Scriptures, engaging in legalism? Is this a legitimate charge against the genuine Christian (granted there are some who hypocritically judge under the moniker of Christ)? Maybe there are times that Christians are legalistic in this area, and the charge of bigotry and lack of charitableness is fitting. It behooves us then to know and understand what is and what is not ambiguous in the area of sexuality, as it is taught in the Word of God.

The ditch on the other side of the road is equally dangerous. It is not good to treat the expressed and clear will of God in direct commands as if they were ambiguous. There is a promise of woe or sorrow to those who call good evil, and who call evil good (Isa 5:20). There is a warning of condemnation from Christ Himself to any who would break the smallest commandments of His law and teach others to do so (Matt 5:19). If we fail to keep the clear commands of the Lord in our life and go about to teach others that it is acceptable for them to do so, we are expressing rebellion against our Lord. Antinomianism, the opposite of grace just like legalism is the opposite of grace, may seem to win friends and even salve consciences, but its error is as bad if not worse than that of the legalist. So, we must know what things are clear in this area.

Another wrinkle in this conversation is the matter of relevance regarding the law itself. Does Old Testament law inform the Christian regarding general morality or sexuality in particular? What place does the law of Moses, the declaration of the prophets, and the other writings which the early Christians saw as Scripture (breathed out by God, I Tim 3:14–17) have in a discussion of sex? Does the New Testament in its declaration of the gospel embrace any of those principles and make them fitting for Christian morality? The red-letter Christians would say that the law has no relevance, only the words of Christ. But Christ honored the law and even made the Torah His starting point for sexual ethics. We know that some parts of the law have passed out of use. We do not go to the temple and offer blood sacrifices. The question then is two-fold. First, we must answer the question of the relevance of Old Testament law on the life of the Christian. Then, we need to see what and how New Testament imperatives apply this to human sexuality.

The proper application of God's law is the only way to truly possess objective morality. Moses, who received the law, is foundational to ethics, even sexual ethics. The Creator and Lord has spoken. To do what is right in one's own eyes does not work. There was once a serial killer who delighted in killing and making things out of the skin and body parts of his victims. He was doing right in his own eyes. To replace the will of the individual with the collective will of many individuals is not any better. One does not have to study history very long to see that the collective will of any society can be corrupted, cruel, and unjust. The transcendent alone, a voice from outside of humanity, can give objective and clear morality, unsoiled by individual self-serving opinion. For both the individual and society, doing what is right in one's own eyes will inevitably lead to moral corruption. That was the way of the ancient Israelites who adopted such a chaotic moral philosophy in the book of Judges. It was not long before Benjamin was indistinguishable from Sodom and Dan was as idolatrous as the Amorites. By the time we come to the end of that book, there is moral chaos. What had merited the righteous judgment of a Holy God was practiced freely among those who were God's people. And Israel as a whole lacked moral clarity on how to correct it. We ignore the law of God, individually and collectively, to our own peril.

But, again, what laws do we claim? The short answer must be all of them, when properly and contextually understood. Even ambiguous laws such as not muzzling the ox that treads the cornfield had righteous moral application that remains applicable to all (Deut 25:4, I Cor 9:9, 10). None of the words of God can be esteemed lightly. But there are obviously some laws that are not meant for us. The book of Deuteronomy, as the second giving of the law, showed earmarks of the fact that some laws were circumstantial as to their letter. The laws that were given in the desert while wandering in the book of Exodus were not exactly the same as the laws given in Deuteronomy, which were meant for the people who were going to settle in the Promised Land. There were, then, things in the giving of the law in Exodus that to the Israelites that settled in the land were no longer relevant outside of their underlying principle. The laws given to Adam are not the laws given to Noah, which are not those given to Moses. These do not necessarily have a one-to-one relevance to those that are under the law to Christ.

Further, there are laws that were specific to the agricultural economy of that day that cannot in our economy be followed with absolute fidelity in the letter. We can seek to learn principles from them that can be applied differently for us. We may not need to leave the corner of our fields unworked in the harvest for the sake of the poor, but we can learn how to make provision in our paychecks to meet the real needs of our neighbors. For the Christian today, we cannot follow the commands for temple worship. There is no temple today and all the sacrificial rites appear to be completely finished in Christ (Heb 9:11–14, 10:1–9). Dietary laws do not seem to be fixed in the Old and New Testaments. The dietary law given to Adam was not the same as what was given to Noah, which was not the same that was given to Moses, which was also not the same that was given to the Christian (Gen 1:29, 9:30, Lev 13, I Tim 4:4, 5). How that looked and how one glorified the Lord in the way that they ate and drank changed. But, the fact that how we eat and drink is part of our worship did not change (I Cor 10:31). We are all worshiping our God in every facet of our life. There is wisdom needed in approaching the law of God to know how to apply it.

We are blessed, though, that we are not the first ones to ask the question of how we today, in the light of the advent of Christ, are supposed to apply the law. The first Jerusalem council in the book of Acts addressed this very thing. Gentiles were being converted to Christ and some desired to teach them that they must become Jewish proselytes, obeying all the ordinances given by Moses in letter, especially starting with the ordinance of circumcision. In other words, they were being told to completely forsake in total the culture of their origin and follow in strict letter all that God commanded Moses (Acts 15:1–5, Gal 2:14). In order to be Christian (that is, in order to be saved or to be sanctified wholly to God), Gentile converts were told to accept the role of Jewish proselytes and begin to live and eat and walk as a Jew under Mosaic law. Paul condemned this as a false gospel, something that relies on the works of the law instead of the faith of Christ (Gal 1:6, 7, 2:14–3:14). The apostles and early elders of the church met to speak about this issue of the law and its relevance to Gentile converts.

There have been many church councils that have been of great value to the church, but this council is the only one that bears the testimony of being inspired by the Spirit of God. Its conclusion was received with joy by all the churches and was marked by the manifestation of the Spirit (Acts 15:24–32, 41). The conclusion of the council was summed up by the apostle James, "Wherefore my sentence is, that we trouble not them, which from among the

Gentiles are turned to God: But that we write unto them, that they abstain from pollutions of idols, and from fornication, and from things strangled, and from blood" (Acts 15:19, 20). Then it was carried to the Gentile churches by Paul, Barnabas, and others by epistle where it was written, "For it seemed good to the Holy Ghost, and to us, to lay upon you no greater burden than these necessary things; That ye abstain from meats offered to idols, and from blood, and from things strangled, and from fornication: from which if ye keep yourselves, ye shall do well" Acts 15:28, 29). This is probably a summary given by Luke, for Paul would later mention the need to remember the provisions of the law regarding the care of the poor, as well (Gal 2:9, 10). But these were the major points and bore repeating by Luke's account in Acts.

This sentence summed up the Gentile expectation to the moral commands of the law of Moses, as they are related to their continued relationship with their culture of origin. It was declared to be the full consensus of apostolic authority, which is the foundation of the church (Eph 2:20). It was claimed to be, being apostolic in its authority, inspired by the Holy Spirit of God. It was reiterated by James a third time in the book of Acts in conversation with Paul (Acts 21:25). The early church saw these points of adherence to the law central to any God-fearing Gentile who named the name of Christ and continue to live and witness for Christ in their culture. Paul himself would declare that as a Jew he would act as a Jew (following all cultural norms of the Jew as to the practical and cultural applications of Mosaic law) and when among Gentiles he would act as a Gentile (following all their cultural norms, norms that were not directly informed by Mosaic law) in order to win those within either culture to Christ (I Cor 9:19–23).

What parts of the law of Moses in strict letter are binding on the Christian as they live and witness for Christ in an immoral culture is therefore summarized by the earliest followers of Christ. We are morally obligated in abstaining from communal and practical forms of idolatry, from a couple specific points of Levitical dietary laws, and expected to follow all laws dealing with sexual morality. That does not mean that we cannot and do not study Moses and the law and find application for us in all areas of life, for they are all profitable to us, especially for our understanding of practical righteousness. There are further parts of the law to which we should allow to shape us. Again, Paul gave testimony that this same discussion of the law included encouragement to be mindful of the poor, which Paul fully supported (Gal 2:9, 10). And we certainly learn more about what it means to not steal by studying Mosaic case law (e.g., Deut 22:1–4). And Paul found practical application to provisions like the muzzling of oxen. The apostles repeatedly showed us we can and should learn from the law. Christ after all is our lawgiver and has given us commands (Matt 28:19). He is the end of the law (Rom 10:4). It means only that the apostles saw this as the summary of laws necessary to observe in strict letter for all believers as they relate to their culture. The Jerusalem Council answered the question for the Gentile believers of how they could be in the world and minster Christ to their culture without being of the world (John 15:19, 17:14–16, I Cor 5:9–11).

Before delving into these words, it should be noted that, while this is generally understood as to its meaning, there were further clarifications as to application. For instance, regarding sexual immorality, Paul had to deal with people who applied this too broadly, teaching that we should not marry, divorced individuals should not be permitted to remarry, and other such prohibitions (I Cor 7). Paul had to correct some overzealousness and even heretical asceticism that came from its over application. The same was so with forbidding to eat meat or buy certain sources of meat (I Tim 4:1–4, II Cor 8). Even these points could be twisted legalistically.

Obviously, the last point regarding sexual immorality is our focus currently, but it behooves the believer to have a cursory understanding of the other points of this judgment as well. Let us take a second and go back to square one regarding law and its relationship to the gospel, though it may seem tedious.

Not that there is ever a change in the truth of the Scriptures. But there is or was an expectation that the law would change. God Himself spoke of the old covenant being done away and a new covenant with His people coming (Jer 31:31–34, Heb 8, 10, II Cor

3). This necessitated a change in the law. There would be a change in the priesthood, a change in the day of rest,[1] a change in the sacrifices, and so on (Heb 7:12, see also chapters 4 and 9). The truth of the law would find its completion and fulfillment in Christ and those things that shadowed Him would be done away. Those who still look legalistically at many of the provisions of the law and cannot see Christ as their end and fulfillment miss the truth of the Scriptures. Something better was coming with Him.

There are things that Christ fulfilled that are outside of the necessity of the Christian to repeat ceremonially, such as sacrifices, temple worship, laws regarding ceremonial cleanliness, etc. Christ fulfilled, once and for all, these things and gave us new ordinances (baptism and the Lord's Supper) to show the fulfillment of those things in Him. We see Christ in our study of those things in the law, but we need not repeat them. They remain as the tutor of men to lead them to Christ (Gal 3:24). He also gave us a new rule by which we live, the Lordship and commands of Christ (Matt. 28:18–20). His rule as Lord does not negate the moral commands of the law, but expand them universally and cause us to rest in Christ for our perfect fulfillment of them. He becomes the absolute pattern of our life. We walk after Him and love as He loved.

Further, there are things in the law that were cultural, pertaining to the agrarian economy in which ancient Israel lived. Pretending to live in the days of old, before electric lights will do nothing for our sanctification. We, again, do not need to worry about keeping the letter of the laws regarding putting fencing around our roof or leaving the corner of our fields unharvested. Most of us do not grow crops or live on the slope of a hillside.

---

1. This is not without controversy but debates about continuity/discontinuity of the law and grace distinction will always have their tensions among us. As to the keeping of the Sabbath versus the keeping of the Lord's Day, all Christians should at least agree that, since Christ has come, we are no longer limited to specific observance of a specific day or time and have entered the perpetual observation of what is called "today" (Heb 4) and have found perfect and permanent sabbath or rest in Christ (Matt 11:28). It is never a sin for Christians to gather on any given day or time and it is always sinful for us to judge one another for such things (Rom 14:1–6).

We can learn principles from these that should be carried over into our moral context, such as caring that our neighbor may be injured by our negligence or caring about using our blessings for the use of those in need. These are the gospel prerogatives that speak of our walk with Christ. In this sense, the law justifies or condemns us in many ways and the law can be summed up in its application as love toward God and love toward our neighbor. The specifics of case law for that period are rarely literally binding in our current context but our study of that case law helps us define the spirit of the law and our moral obligations before God. Going back again to Paul, for instance, inferring from the law about the muzzling of the ox, a Christian has a moral obligation for caring for those that labor among them, which is established by our reading of the law of God (Deut 25:4, I Cor 9:9, I Tim 5:18). If we were to demand a strict adherence to the letter of that law, we would all need to own property, own oxen, and use those oxen to plow our fields. And there would only be a need for us to care for that one specific ox. It would be folly to think that a Christian farmer is under moral obligation to never buy or use a tractor. There is no need to believe that we need to go to such extreme cultural and economic changes in order to obey the commands of God. We can however be instructed by the law on how we care for those that do work on our behalf. We honor Christ by seeking to live His law.

There are also things in the law that were specific commands of God in the context of that time that were not binding outside of the Jews in that historical setting. There are aspects of the law that would not bind the Christian, though they would have instructive force. For instance, God commanded Israel to go to war and conquer Canaan. Would we have parallels to our spiritual sanctification? Sure! But we have no command of God to conquer anything in our physical context. There are also laws within the Torah that were obviously not sufficiently moral outside of the context of Israel being set aside as holy by God and that truth is made obvious by those laws not making up the litany of reasons that God judged nations outside of Israel. We know, without getting ahead of ourselves, that sexual immorality and idolatry were things for which

45

God judged and destroyed nations outside of Israel, meaning that those things had a wider and already understood moral scope than just the Israeli context (Lev 18). The nations outside of Israel knew in their consciences that sexual immorality and idolatry were evil. However, there is nothing in the law that shows that God held the rest of humanity responsible for keeping specific laws of the sabbath, dietary laws, laws of ceremony, etc. For instance, God did not judge Sodom for wearing clothing of mixed types of material or sowing their fields with mixed types of seeds. God did expect all of humanity to worship Him alone and not turn to foolish idols, to do justice, to care for the needy, to maintain sexual purity, etc.

The consensus of the early church, codified by apostolic authority and the authentication of the Holy Spirit, was that Christian liberty in the truth of all that Christ had accomplished was to be proclaimed. For liberty we were called to Christ and not to any bondage to things Christ has fulfilled (Gal 5:1). The keeping of the law in all its ceremonies and types and rites had come to an end in Christ. But. Christian liberty did not render the law inoperative. It still speaks with absolute moral authority. The law would not allow Christian licentiousness. There can be no Christian antinomianism (lawlessness). The Christian was without the law only in a sense that they were under the law to Christ (I Cor 9:21). They were now under His absolute Lordship to follow His commands. And when their Lord spoke, He spoke from the moral context of the law and did not abdicate any of its moral authority. In fact, the Sermon on the Mount showed that He gave greater authority to the law. When He spoke of the command not to kill, He did not diminish its moral authority but gave it a deeper meaning (Matt 5:21, 22). He was the Lawgiver. When the law was given, it was the Son that gave it. When He was asked about marriage, He referred to Moses and expounded its moral implications (Matt 5:27–32). Through the law is the knowledge of sin (Rom 3:20). The law therefore stands as a moral bulwark upon which the truths of the gospel stand. Christ came to save sinners (I Tim 1:15). And Christ came declaring law. The law tells us with an unmistakable voice that we are guilty sinners deserving the full and final punishment of the law. And in Christ we are to not continue in sin (I John 3:9).

Again, there is no room for antinomianism within Christian liberty. The apostles at the Jerusalem Council highlighted three areas where the law was to absolutely limit Christian liberty. First, there was to be no place for idolatry among Christians. Do not eat things, partake of things, belonging to false gods. "Little children, keep yourselves from idols" (I John 5:21). The first table of the law still belongs to us (no other gods, no graven images, no using His name with vanity, keeping the day unto Him holy). And no view of Christian liberty makes idolatry acceptable Christian behavior. The Gentiles must submit wholly to the law here regardless of their political or familial culture that inundate them. Your culture may excuse idolatry, but your God does not. They may not need to be circumcised and observe things fitting to the Jewish culture, but they sure could not continue in the idolatry of the Gentiles with Christ as their Lord.

The apostles and the early church said that Gentiles were not to eat meat offered to idols or rather were to keep themselves from the pollution of idols. Paul pointed out that there could be an over-legalistic and uncharitable application even to this. There could be brothers who are unjustly condemned for buying affordable meat because of possible unknown practices of the meat market-ers obtaining cheaper shambles of meat from pagan temples and reselling it (I Cor 10:25). There were Christians that were unfairly condemned for attending social events because of the possible, yet unknown, sources of the meat served (I Cor 10:27). That was cor-rected by the Spirit through the writings of the apostles. However, there was to be no intentional reverence given to any idol actively or passively. "Ye cannot drink the cup of the Lord, and the cup of devils: ye cannot be partakers of the Lord's table, and of the table of devils" (I Cor 10:21). So, attend your family events, eat what is set before you. But, if it is made known at any time that the meat is for the purpose of idolatrous practice, abstain.

When the law speaks of idolatry, we should hear what it says even when it comes practically to our everyday mundane activities.

There are definite idolatrous practices that were condemned by the law that break the first table of the law. To ignore those is to be condemned by the law justly. God has judged nations and will yet judge nations and individuals for their idolatry. "But I say, that the things which the Gentiles sacrifice, they sacrifice to devils, and not to God: and I would not that ye should have fellowship with devils" (I Cor 10:20). The Christian cannot sit in fellowship with those that are giving reverence to anything less than God. They cannot consent that anything other than God can be adored. There is no New Testament command that would free the believer to the practice of any form of idolatry or to fellowship with any in that end. Like Daniel, they cannot defile themselves with the King's meat (Dan. 1:8). They could not pinch the incense and say Caesar is Lord. As the temple of the Lord, we must be holy, holy unto our Lord.

And the apostles also marked out a dietary law of sorts for Christians in liberty. Christians are obligated to be convinced by their Lord wholly in this matter, whatever they may choose to eat for the glory of God, but cannot obligate or judge others in this matter (Rom 14:1–6). But they are not, by the judgment of the apostles, to eat the blood and or to eat things that are strangled. The original dietary law under the Adamic covenant was the herb of the field (Gen 1:29). On the other side of the judgment of the flood a change in the law came with the Noahic covenant to allow the eating of all meat (Gen 9:3). Then the law of Moses, under the Mosaic covenant, was brought forth with specific commands for Israel (note again, no nation was ever judged by God for failure to keep the dietary law given by Moses to Israel). The strictness of diet served to make the people of God holy or separated unto their God (see Leviticus 11). The implication of the words of the apostles is that there is an abdication of those dietary laws for the Gentile believer or even the Jewish believer that is so convinced (But I will not dictate to any person's conscience here, Rom 14:23). It marked a return to the post-judgment diet given to Noah, a blessing for a people who are inheriting the earth. Every living thing is your meat but do not eat the blood (Gen 9:3, 4). This is fitting, since the Christian, like Noah in type, has passed through the judgment of God in Christ upon sin. On the other side of the cross, we eat in liberty. We can no longer call anything unclean, as was taught in type to Peter (Acts 10:13, 14). Paul was convinced of this truth (Rom 14:14). We can receive all with thanksgiving to God. Speaking against those that would forbid meat, Paul said, "For every creature of God is good, and nothing to be refused, if it be received with thanksgiving: For it is sanctified by the word of God and prayer" (I Tim 4:4, 5).

But we cannot wholly set aside the principles of the law, even in the smallest matters such as our diet. We are called upon by the Holy Ghost, and the apostles He inspired, to recognize two things that were prescribed by the law in our eating. These principles pre-dated the law of Moses to give us continuity between Moses and Noah who came before him. The principle is that of respecting the life of that thing which we eat. The life of the flesh is in the blood (Lev 17:11). To eat with the blood may be related to idolatrous practice and therefore connected with the first prohibition. It is more likely simply the idea that we are to humanely kill and drain the blood in respect for the life we are taking. The idea of things strangled and eating blood go together. Things that are killed inhumanely by means other than a simple shedding of the blood are to be refused. The men of Saul fell upon the sheep and ate them without taking time to prepare them (I Sam 14:32, 33). And we are not to eat that which is not living, that is the idea of avoiding things strangled. Dead things are not to be our meat (Gen 9:3, 4). If we find something dead we do not make it our meat. It is the living things that become our meat and we are to care to humanely and carefully take their life and then use their substance for our sustenance. The things in the law that give greater light on this, should be heard. There is a sense in the law that the issue of blood had a recognition of God allowing the life of the animal to be given for us to live. The draining of the blood was then a purposeful recognition of that truth (Deut 12:15, 16, Lev 17:12, 13). All our food is received with thanksgiving. The principle leads into the instruction of the Lord's Table, where we see the blood separated from the meat representing a life, the life, having been given for us and received as such with thanksgiving (Matt 26:26–28, John 6:54, 55). Whether we eat or drink, we do all to the glory of our God (I Cor 10:31).

The points of idolatry and diet (fidelity toward God and care for the creature He gave us) are not, however, the focus of this present discussion. They do demonstrate the general relevance of the law and need of reverence by the Christian to what God has spoken in it. All things are yet under His commandments, even if our application of it has differed. The last aspect of the law that the apostles declared to be binding on the Christian is laws regarding sexual purity. Keep yourselves from fornication or rather from all forms of sexual immorality.

Paul, again, would be led by the Holy Spirit to correct some abuses of this imperative. There were some with heretical proto-Gnostic teachings that defined all sex as immoral and began to forbid people to marry (I Tim 4:3). That was an excessive prohibition. There can be an overly legalistic interpretation to God's law whether from Judaizing or Gnostic influences. Notwithstanding, the word fornication has a very clear meaning in terms of the law and was very clearly defined by the apostles after this point. Does the law when it speaks of sexual morality pertain to the Christian? Here, in the Jerusalem Council, the answer is emphatically affirmative.

There is a sense in which the determination of the Jerusalem Council was a repudiation of pagan culture. Sex was a central focus of pagan temple worship along with the eating of things offered to idols. Pagan worship had as a central tenant the celebration of sexual orgies in order to make contact with their gods and appease those gods. The determination of the Jerusalem Council focused on the proper place of food and sexuality in terms of Christian worship. Those that limit the prohibitions of sexual immorality to pagan temple liturgy fail to see the all encompassing life of worship for God's people. We worship in all we do. We are God's temple. The Council was repudiating that culture without burdening Gentile believers in having to embrace Jewish culture, with laws regarding cleanness and such like. Only two, possibly three, of the Ten Commandments, are in any way connected with sexual morality (Do not commit adultery, do not covet, and, in a roundabout way, honor your parents). This does not repudiate the remaining commandments (do not steal, kill, or bear false witness). Those commandments are consistently reiterated in the New Testament and carry weight, even greater weight, under the economy of Christ. And our understanding of the application of all of them are expounded by Old Testament law. Gentile believers were not asking the apostles to judge whether they were now able to kill or steal. They were asking if they needed to change their diet and cultural practices in order to follow Christ. This was not an antinomian question. And the apostles affirmed their liberty in Christ and defeated legalistic misapplications of the law.

The apostles were not intending to prescribe and exegete all the moral law to the Gentile converts. There was no need to tell them that murder, theft, or perjury were evil. Their culture understood such laws to be just. Their culture, however, did not consider drunken idolatrous reveling, banqueting, and orgies to be morally wrong and the pronouncement of the council addressed that in all its parts. It was intended to answer the question on what parts of the law were relevant for converts to keep *in contradiction to their prevailing culture*. One side was saying that these converts must be circumcised and then keep the law of Moses in its entirety without any deference to what was fulfilled by Christ; all the laws of cleanness, all the feasts and observations and convocations, all the sacrifices, were all said to be necessary to having a right relationship with God (Acts 15:1–5). They were saying that Jewish culture must be completely embraced. The opposing Christian view was that none of that is necessary to the Christian made free by Christ (see this tension in Rom 14:1–6). He was their circumcision, He was their Sabbath, He was their Passover, He was their atonement and means of cleansing, and so on. That is the view of liberty in Christ and that, by the direction of the Holy Spirit through apostolic authority, won the day.

This did not mean that the law of Moses was set aside. Those converts needed to be sexually pure before God, just as they needed (in the tradition of the law) to be mindful of glorifying God in the most mundane issues, like their diet, and to be mindful to not give any reverence to false gods, even in culturally accepted practices. This is a worldview shift for them, there is one Lord and that Lord is recognized in all we do (I Cor 8:4–6).

The prohibition against sexual immorality codified the idea that the law speaks authoritatively on sexual morality. Here now it stands written as a fact. Though not an exhaustive statement on the relationship between the Christian and the Law, it is a specific and exact one. What Moses wrote by the inspiration of God about sexual morality is fully binding for all who call on Christ, and, since Christ is judge of all, it is binding for all in this present evil world. Laws about sex are cross-cultural. Going back to this idea of what God did and did not judge nations for in the past, the majority of the things that God through Moses revealed that He judged nations for, outside of idolatrous practices, were issues of sexual morality. Things such as incest relationships (Lev 18:4–18), not setting aside as unclean sex during menstruation (Lev 18:19), adultery (Lev 18:20), infanticide (Lev 18:21), having same sex relationships (Lev 18:22), and human beings have sex with animals (Lev 18:23) were listed as abominable things that God brought judgment upon, regardless of nation, cultural norms, or ethnicity (Lev 18:24–29). Therefore, God taught the cross-cultural truth of these moral laws.

All of these are understandably under the heading of fornication. Take the matter of incest. Paul called on the church in Corinth to address fornication among them, namely that a man was having sex with his father's wife (I Cor 5). The understanding that that was sinful was based on Old Testament law from the book of Leviticus, given to Israel and declared to be applicable beyond the borders of Israel. What the Scriptures, Old and New Testament have to say about the subject of sex is relevant to all, especially all who name the name of Christ. If one limits themselves only to the red letters of Christ, or what is reiterated in the New Testament from the Old, they would be unable to define sexual immorality. The underlying principles are found in the Law and the prophets.

No matter how much the culture embraces sexual immorality, they are embracing evil condemned by God's law. What is sexually immoral is defined by God and not by culture. The word usually translated as fornication in Hebrew is equivalent in the Old Testament with both idolatry and adultery. For instance, Ezekiel blasted the Israelites for fornication in going after other gods when they were married or by covenant joined to Him (Ezek 16). Adultery is therefore a form of fornication. In fact, faithful marriage is the spiritual and physical ideal as created by God and all spiritual and physical departures from that are sexually immoral. Thus, Christ could expound that a married man lusting after a woman that is not his wife is already guilty of adultery (Matt 5:27, 28). He could also expound that fornication is the breaking of one's marriage vows and legitimate cause for divorce (Matt 5:31, 32). The fornication of Gomar against Hosea was analogous to the idolatry of Israel against her God (Hosea 1–3). Jude proclaimed that Sodom stood forth us as an example of God's judgment against fornication in their going after strange flesh (pointing to the biblical data of the men of the city desiring to have sex and even rape the men that came to the house of Lot, Jude 1:7). Paul, as was already noted, equated laws of incest with fornication (I Cor 5:1). He also equated the physical and spiritual acts of Israel with the Moabites as fornication (I Cor. 10:8, Num. 25:1–9). This seems to have been the commentary of John of the same incident, in condemnation of practices in the church being established in contradiction to the declaration of the Jerusalem Council, "thou hast there them that hold the doctrine of Balaam, who taught Balac to cast a stumblingblock before the children of Israel, to eat things sacrificed unto idols, and to commit fornication" (Rev. 2:14).

Paul taught directly that fornication is a sin we commit with and against our own bodies (I Cor 6:18). Any attempt to spiritualize these ideas is futile. Any attempt to Gnosticize them and say I can be a good spiritual person and still use my body for sex outside of biblical marriage in disregard of the declarations of the law is likewise futile. What we do in our bodies is done in an absolute moral context. It is a context in which God at various times and in various ways has spoken as Lord concerning. This creates a real antithesis of right and wrong, good and evil in all sexual acts or thoughts that we engage in. A Christian cannot simply act as if God has not spoken on the issue of sex. And neither can the non-Christian twist the words of the Scriptures to say the Scriptures teach otherwise.

Again, everyone that exists acts in an absolute moral context. This context is not created by them and the value of the things that they choose is not subjective. There are things that they may choose that are good and there are things that they may choose that are evil. This moral tension is experienced in the conscience of every person. They know the simple truth and the guilt that comes from it, they live in a reality in which God has spoken. And God shall bring those deeds into judgment and will judge them by the things written in His books (Rev. 20:11–15).

The Soteriology of Sex

Antithesis 4: Those Who are Lost and Those Who are Saved

"And such were some of you . . . ." First Corinthians 6:14

OUR CONTEMPORARIES WOULD EQUATE sex and salvation in a much different way than the biblical authors have done. To our contemporaries, absolute sexual liberty is the only acceptable ethic, and the orgasm is the grand means of experiencing salvation. Sex is freedom. Sex is heaven. Sex is life. Sex is a means of overthrowing the shackles of patriarchy and a puritanical morality (by which they mean Christ and His law). These are the maxims of the sexual revolution. To have a sexually positive life is to be beyond shame and guilt, to achieve wholeness by acting beyond the categories of right and wrong, good and evil. Before, in their view, one experiences the liberation of sex they are repressed. It, in the words of Peter, promises them liberty (II Pet 2:19). It promises joy. Sex, as it is advertised, can give you all things that you want and need. Therefore, every product in the marketplace seems to promise sex if you buy the product. Therefore, in a sex-centered politic, sex should be free, without boundaries, without limits, without judgments, and without consequence. It is the means of salvation to the repressed, who have no desire for God in their bedroom or public discourse, unless God fully affirms all their desires. These, our contemporaries, are without God and have no hope outside of the fleeting present moment and its physical sensations. Everything for them, in an enduring Freudian sense, is about sex.

Is this real though? Do the advertising taglines about sexuality live up to their promises or do they create buyer's remorse? Is sex, that is sex outside of God's expressed will, salvation or fodder for judgment? Does it bring health or guilt? What does it say about the God who is truly there and our relationship to that Most High God?

The Christian must presuppose two points about the subject of sexuality, and with all broader points of human activity. First, the reality of sex is an artifact of the Creator/creature distinction. As such, God is Lord over sex as a concept and all practices that spring from it. He has created it, interpreted it, and has given it meaning and purpose. Everything that happens in the realm of human sexuality is to be submitted to and must be ready to answer to Him as Lord. Secondly, the Christian presupposes the fact that the Lord has made His will concerning sexual activity known by the revelation of Himself. He has revealed His truth in nature and has revealed His will by means of His commandments. God as Lord prevents us from interpreting sexuality based on our own reasoning or desires. We submit to His Lordship. The Lord as lawgiver, keeps us from behaving sexually based only on what we want to do. We live and act in a reality where we are morally bound to do as our Lord has commanded. These are biblical presuppositions and are well founded in reality. To deny them is to embrace ethical and metaphysical chaos where nothing can be affirmed universally. The Christian offers to the world Logos, the world that rejects the Christian message rather chooses to embrace Chaos.

As such, our sexual behavior necessarily speaks, not just of our relationship with the object of our desire, but of our relationship with the Lord. To understand how this matter of sexuality speaks more broadly of our relationship with God, it is necessary to understand the nature of sin. It is easy in contemporary culture to get lost in the minutia of politics about sex. 'Do you think there is something wrong with X?' The political environment forces people to qualify every statement with nuance so as to not offend or make oneself look bigoted. The spiritual questions however should always be focused on what God is pleased with. A broader point is the moral question, 'Is there such a thing as sin?' 'Is there anything ultimately wrong with anything we do?' 'Is the guilt of our sin real?' 'Is there going to be a judgment of the things that we do in and with our bodies?' Arbitrary opinion is meaningless if any of these questions are affirmed. If there is sin, it should be shunned. If there is guilt, an atonement should be sought. If there is final judgment, it should be feared.

The question from the beginning was centered on this matter of authority. As Creator, God is Lord and could freely limit any part of His creation. The raging waves have their stopping point at His commandment (Job 38:11). As such, the Lord gave law. There was only one law in the beginning, and that law had nothing to do with sex, or personal property, or any other periphery thing. It had to do with the authority of God as Lord and Creator to limit the liberty of His creation. Thus, one single commandment was given in the light of perfect freedom. Of every tree mankind could freely eat, except for one. Mankind could otherwise continue in perfect productivity in a perfect environment, enjoying without shame all the joys of this world, even sexual pleasure.

Mankind was not content to remain under the authority of the command of the Lord. It all began by allowing that authority to be questioned, "Did God really say?" It proceeded from doubt to a challenge of the command itself, a perceived right of man to question God. They presumed that they could themselves judge between the authoritative end, "you will surely die" as weighed against the claim made to its antithesis, "you will not surely die." Vaulting themselves to a position of final arbiter of all claims of truth, they decided that the command of God could be broken. They saw that this thing was forbidden to them by God. They judged for themselves that it appeared to be just as good for food as any other tree they are allowed to freely eat from. They judged that the fruit was aesthetically pleasing, it enticed their appetite and there should be nothing that suppressed the appetite. Then they judged for themselves the consequences, if they took from this fruit they would become as gods themselves. They would have the authority; they would assert their right to know and experience good and evil for themselves. Thus, the fateful decision was made; they forsook the authority and Lordship of their Creator. They took the fruit in full rebellion. And we have lived under the real consequences of that since that chaotic day.

One cannot simply ignore the authority of the Lord and have a right relationship with Him. There is a sense in which humanity has been held back by grace. They did not die that day in the sense of entering into final judgment against their sin. They continued to live, to reproduce, and to eat. The longsuffering of God against sinners began that day, as rebels against God were allowed to continue on in creation with judgment being suspended for a time. There is also a sense in which they did die. They came out of the other side of their rebellious choice separated from their God, who was their life. They emerged dead in trespasses and sins (Eph 2:1). Mankind was now held by the chains of their sin and condemned justly already before their God (John 3:18).

This separation from their God, or this death, is seen in three lights. They were *unclean* in their own sight. They, for the first time, saw themselves as naked and were ashamed. They began to try to cover up the shame of their nakedness. But, all their efforts to do so were to no avail. They were *unholy*. They were unable to stand in the presence of their Lord. They were no longer unto or for Him. Hiding behind bushes, they scurried away from the voice of the Lord, hoping to avoid His sight. They were afraid. They were *guilty*. When addressing the issue of their own unholiness and uncleanness before God, they had to answer the question before the judgment seat of their God, "did you eat of the fruit that you were commanded not to eat?" All attempts to shift the blame of their choice failed and they were found guilty before their God. And we all were there in them in all of this (Rom 5:12–19). In Adam, all die (I Cor 15:22). This is our shared human experience.

Sin may promise liberty, but it produces guilt. It may promise meaning, but it produces unholiness, no longer being unto a greater end. It may promise happiness, but it produces a deep sense of uncleanness. Setting aside the eschatological matter of what sin means after this life, there is a profound implication of the soteriological impact of sin upon us now. Salvation is of the Lord and the partaking of sin forsakes its own salvation. Sin declares an allegiance with that which is opposed to God. The one that practices sin is of the devil and not one that is born of God (I John 3:7–10). Sin, therefore, declares a relationship and an allegiance. In a world obsessed with identity politics, sin is a declaration of who we really are in a relationship to our God.

Further, the sins one tends to pursue also tends to form a character in them. To take part in a sin once, makes it harder to resist partaking in that same thing a third or fourth time. A child that steals a piece of gum at the store is easily tempted to try again. As they continue to do so, the activity becomes ingrained in their character. They are now thieves. The one who sins is a servant or rather a slave of that sin (John 8:34). And our relationship to that sin becomes an identifying mark of our character.

The Scriptures are replete with examples of those who bear the character of their sin. All liars shall have their part in the lake of fire (Rev 21:8). The term liar there is a description of character. In that same context, titles like idolater and murderer are used as character names to describe the sins by which those persons have become and will then be known. They are verbal categories that describe the bent of that person. One can be known by their pet sinful activities. One can be called proud or self-righteous by that same sentiment, and they often are in the Scriptures. While there is not much that can be said for expressive individualism,[1] there is a sense in which it is true. What you think in your heart is what you practice in your actions and will become the character which you display in the world. And that character will be owned on the day of judgment when all are judged according to their works.

Soren Kierkegaard spoke of the base aesthetic life of the Don Juan like character. They are known for living completely to

---

1. The idea of self-creation by which one creates themselves in their own mind by their own desires and then is free to express such in society as the outworking of their liberty and right to define themselves.

themselves without thought of ethical and transcendent categories. As empty as that seems to have been to Kierkegaard, there are many that put the entire stock of their life in seeking that life of pleasure. Our entire culture is consumed with such an aesthetic. This aesthetic naturally finds its home in the outworking of sexual lust. There is an illusion that there is something good or beautiful about seeking and living a life of pleasure, seeking beauty for the sake of beauty itself, as Oscar Wilde would advocate. People will freely define themselves in the terms of their sexual desires, will seek to be known by what they do or desire to do sexually, and will do so openly and proudly believing it to be central to their identity.

The Scriptures will also use such an aesthetic to describe sexual identity but will do so with a different force. One is known by their fruits and by those fruits they are judged (Matt 7:15–20). This is the exact truth that the sexual liberation movement wants to avoid, the idea that what we do reveals what we are and what we are is subject to judgment by the Lord of all. If what we do occurs in a moral context, then it is to be judged. It is either sinful or righteous. If sin is not a real category, then what we do is meaningless, which conclusion is outrageous to our senses. If sin and righteousness however are real categories, then what we do has meaning. This is a fearful conclusion. I do what my heart desires to do and it speaks loudly of the condition of my heart before the one true God before whom I stand.

All the various types of sin brand us. We make ourselves slaves to the sins we commit, and they brand their mark on us conspicuously. "Know ye not, that to whom ye yield yourselves servants to obey, his servants ye are to whom ye obey; whether of sin unto death, or of obedience unto righteousness" (Rom 6:16)? We become known by the character of our sins. A man that is dishonest becomes known as a liar, the man that kills as a murderer. Christ Himself at the end would call people at His judgment workers of iniquity in the vocative sense of direct address. It is the name of their character. It is their branding. It is, in the final accounting, what can be truly said about them.

Sexual sins, like Hawthorne's *Scarlet Letter*, bear a spiritual mark of character upon those that give themselves over to them. The one that sins sexually, sins against their own body (I Cor 6:18). Such ones intermingle and entangle themselves with a greater evil and become one with it (I Cor 6:16). There is a connection in the Scriptures between the concept of idolatry (the worship of a false god) and adultery. Paul connected the covetousness of sexual lust to the sin of idolatry. "Mortify therefore your members which are upon the earth; fornication, uncleanness, inordinate affection, evil concupiscence, and covetousness, which is idolatry . . . " (Col 3:5). In fact, that is a major theme that runs from one cover to another cover of the Scriptures. Can we take the members of Christ, those things that belong to Christ, and make those things members of a harlot and one with it (I Cor 6:16)? Having been made one with or purposed unto Christ, do we then turn and make ourselves one with a harlot? Our sanctification unto God is doing the will of God, in body and in spirit (I Cor 6:19, 20). It demands that we maintain these vessels (our physical bodies) in sanctification and honor (I Thess 4:3, 4). Our bodies are not for the uncleanness of sexual immorality but to be used in accordance with the will of God. Our body has a Lord and is purposed for our Lord. When we give ourselves over to sexual sins, we declare unfaithfulness to God. We despise His will.

Now, these concepts apply to those who are the people of God, but they demonstrate the broader truth. No one can be sexually immoral without stating loudly with their very lives that they are opposed to God. Their sin becomes the mark of their character. How do you describe one opposed to God, one that is lost? You can describe them in the terms of the sin that they chose against, or in opposition to, God. Whatever that thing is, it is their chief idol which they worship and ultimately become like. "They that make [idols or false gods] are like unto them; so is every one that trusteth in them" (Ps 115:8). What will it profit a man to gain the world and lose his own soul (Mark 8:36). "Behold," we might say, "This one here plotted, strove, and often obtained their deepest desires and what did it gain them?" Written over that character is the ominous truth, "these shall not inherit the kingdom of God" (I Cor 6:9, 10)! These are not of God. Their works deny Him. Some may be deceived in believing that they can give themselves fully to sin and still lay claim to the things of God. This deception is deep. This deception has many advocates. But we stand before God and His commands alone. "For whosoever shall keep the whole law, and yet offend in one point, he is guilty of all" (James 2:10).

The sexually immoral person is proclaiming by their life that they are lost and have no part with God. That truth should make them tremble. Paul again stated, "Know ye not that the unrighteous shall not inherit the kingdom of God? Be not deceived: fornicators . . . shall [not] inherit the kingdom of God." There is more there but let us pause to focus on the sin of sexual immorality in general, the fornicator. Those that generally practice their sinful sexual desires are lost and inherit nothing of God in their end. The whole world may help them in their deception, telling them they are alright, but though hand joins in hand the wicked will not escape their judgment (Prov 11:21). Sexual purity does not save, but sexual licentiousness is a witness to the condition of one's lostness. This is something I beg the reader to ponder.

Also, "Be not deceived: adulterers . . . shall [not] inherit the kingdom of God." That, according to Christ, would include that lustfulness and wantonness that describes many in society (Matt 5:27, 28). There are those whose eyes are full of adultery (II Pet 2:14). And so, it is with, as in the King James language, the effeminate (*malakos*, a word to describe a male who carries themselves in an effeminate way, or is even used sexually by another male as if they were feminine). So it is with, again in the King James English, abusers of themselves with mankind (*arsenokoites*, a compound word that describes a male that does with another male in bed what they would do with a female, the unnatural use of Rom 1). These acts of sexual immorality are not meant to be an exhaustive list of all possible sexual sins. They are historically the most prevalent in any culture, especially in ours. But when a person has given themselves over to the practice of these sins (or others of like character outside of the holy bounds set by their Lord) they show themselves to have a character that is opposed to the rule of God. They have no inheritance from God, no standing with Him. They worship something else. They can deceive themselves into believing they do have God, or millions of fellow sinners may be affirming what that they do, but as long as they continue in those sins without godly sorrow and repentance toward God, they display plainly that they are not heirs of God's kingdom. They are not among those who are under God's rule.

Again, this deception runs deep. Recently, an artist wrote a hit song about their sexual sin, describing it as an act of worship, like going to church. The most doglike acts were risen to a place of holy service by the sacrilege. Perverseness in sexual acts is now liturgical. Some will not go as far as making their sexual acts sacraments of their self-centered faith, replacing the one true God with the idol of sexuality, they rather will continue to profess God with their mouths while they deny Him with their works (Titus 1:16). There is a Gnostic kind of Christian heresy that strains at distinctions between the spiritual and the physical. Being spiritual to them is a fuzzy spiritual feeling that does not need to be or cannot be defined, but has nothing to do with what they do with their body. But the deeds of the body will be judged. Their Lord, regardless of their denial, had something to say in that area. They go about in sexual immorality and perverseness deceiving themselves that the Christian or spiritual label can lay claim to the kingdom, all the while acting treasonous against His rule.

What do they get in this state of deception? It is not the promise of the kingdom they receive. That, absent true repentance, is and will be withheld from them. The forbidden fruit did not give them the godhood advertised. "While they promise them liberty, they themselves are the servants of corruption: for of whom a man is overcome, of the same is he brought in bondage" (2 Pet 2:19). There is a spiritual toll to pay. There are wages to sin, a reward for unrighteousness (Rom 6:23). It is not liberation but bondage. If one was to get beyond the facade of the rainbow fig leaf covering, bondage is the most prevalent feature of the sexual revolution aesthetic.

There is guilt that one incurs, a real guilt that finds its impact in one's life apart from their media presence. The sexual sinner is far more likely to struggle with negative feelings of self-worth, depression, cognitive dissonance, psychosis, and suicidal ideation. Self-deception comes at a price. Higher rates of alcohol and substance misuse cannot drown out the persistent voice of guilt and shame. That is just the psychological toll. The social toll may come with an even higher price tag. Absent transcendent purpose, sexual sins have a corrupting influence on everything. Sexual sins destroy the meaning of our relationships. They turn people into objects, love to lust, pleasure to violence and pain, and leave a long line of broken lives and broken homes. And when the thought of God enters the mind, a deep sense of rejection permeates the sinner, and causes them to run from the light and invent new gods after their own image to try to make their actions acceptable.

However, those who are saved were at one time in the same condition as all who are lost. But that ceased to be their state when they were brought under the rule of God. Paul went on to say, "And such *were* some of you: but ye are washed, but ye are sanctified, but ye are justified in the name of the Lord Jesus, and by the Spirit of our God." The Christian is not a morally superior person, but those that once were known by their sins just as others. They were walking after such things and objects of wrath as all others (Eph 2:1–3). But God changed everything for them, grace converted them (Eph 2:4–10). They were that but they are now this. Those changes address the three great needs of the sinner. The sinner is unclean but they have been *washed* by their Lord. The sinner was unholy but found *sanctification* from the Lord. The sinner was guilty but found *justification* from the Lord. These are three specific changes that are highlighted by Paul for those in sin, to include sexual sins; from unclean to clean, from unholy to sanctified, from guilty to justified.

To repeat, the state of the sinner was at one point the condition of all who are saved. The only material difference between the two is the grace of God. One remains in the bondage of their sins and the other is brought mercifully under the rule of God. Take courage! The state of the sinner is not immutable, not beyond the hope of change. Christ is able to cause them to pass from the state of death to the state of life (John 5:24). And there is therefore hope for all who see the misery of their state to be transitioned by the grace of God to something new. If anyone is found in Christ, they are new creations (II Cor 5:17).

First, Christ by His grace is able to take the sinner from being unclean to being clean. The unspoken truth of sexual sins is the knowledge of being unclean. No sooner is the act of sin brought to a close, this reality sets heavy on the bodies and consciences of those who engage in that act. The excitement of the act of sin in the moment pushes away the thought of contamination from the act. All the sinner can think of at the moment is their own satisfaction. Afterwards comes the feeling of contamination. Lady MacBeth could not wash away the murderous spot on her from the killing of King Duncan, no matter how much she cried out for the spot to be removed. Pilate may have tried to wash his hands of the blood of Christ but could not. The desire to be clean is a human desire rooted deep in our consciences. It is a feeling that betrays the consciousness of God. Peter saw himself as unclean in the presence of the holy Christ (Luke 5:8). So did Isaiah in the presence of the thrice Holy (Isa 6:5). The awareness of spiritual contamination is the awareness of a morally pure standard, one that is seeing and judging us, and before whom we are deeply stained.

The folly of sexual sins is that it works contrary to that desire. The sexual sinner cannot help to, after the act, feel physically dirty, and cannot by bathing take that feeling away. It is in them and not something that can simply be washed off. A psychological term of mental contamination can be used to describe this feeling of not just being outwardly dirty but inwardly dirty as well. There is a feeling of shame and disgust at what one just allowed themselves to do and a desire for that shame and disgust to be removed. It is common in illicit acts for the sinner to come cognitively into the grips of regret soon after the moment of pleasure slips away. Only rebellious forms of cognitive dissonance can for a time drive the guilt away, but not without cost and not permanently. The feeling of being unclean is not just reserved for the act of sex. Feelings of being unclean are felt by those who are engaged in the thought of evil. This is the immediate sting of the conscience. The feeling is at the surface level self-directed and self-concerned. In other words, it is concerned with how one sees themselves in the light of their own standards and expectations of self. One expects that they are good and then they get a glimpse of themselves vulnerable, using and being used, base, without honor, without commitment, selfish, and so on.

Attempts to take away the feeling of uncleanness come in the form of rejecting or hating the person that did the act with them, rejecting the moral or religious context that makes them feel dirty, or engaging in self-destructive behavior to try to drown out the feeling (e.g., intoxication). But no matter how many people one hurts, how many moral or religious altars are destroyed, or how much one drowns the memories of what they had done, the feeling of wallowing in the moral mire like a pig never leaves them (II Pet 2:22). Whether it is sexual acts only performed in the mind or acted on in the real physical world, the spot it leaves is not easily ignored and impossible to successfully wash away by their own efforts. Mankind in forgetting their God goes about to defile their bodies among one another (Rom 1:24). The stain is deep and has entered even unto their very conscience (Titus 1:15). As such, they long for a cleansing that no earthly means can reach. Even infamous sinners like Oscar Wilde died asking for a priest.

However, what is not possible for men is possible with God (Matt 19:26). That is the clear soteriology of Scriptures, salvation is a work only God is able to perform. Salvation is of the Lord (Jonah 2:8). Thus, the passive reading of the verb,[2] you were washed. It was not an act you were able to perform yourself. It is a monergistic work of God. It is a deeper washing that is intended here. By nature, we could not cleanse ourselves and remain thus. The nature of the pig is to wallow in the mire and the nature of the dog is to eat its own vomit, but God can change the nature of

---

2. Technically, it is in the middle voice in Greek but naturally read as passive in context.

what we are. The Christian is not morally superior to the lost. The only difference between the sexual sinner and the Christian is that the Christian has been washed, *apolouo*. The reference by Paul is a complete and total washing. Paul was using language that was once told to him when he was yet a murderer and had the blood of the saints on his hands (Acts 22:16). He was told in such a state to commit himself to Christ by being baptized and in so doing to wash away his sins. Peter was quick to say of baptism that the saving was not in the washing of the flesh but in the answer of a good conscience before God (I Pet 3:21). The washing pictured by baptism is the answer of what is pictured (the death, burial, and resurrection of Christ for our sins) and is sufficient to make us clean as a completed act. We are washed from our sins by the work of the Holy Spirit making us new, the washing of regeneration and renewing of the Holy Ghost (Titus 3:5).

The point is that there is a means of washing for every sinner. That means is the gospel of Christ and our complete dependence on that. The believer in Christ was once the character of a defiled person, even the sexually defiled, but will forever sing that Christ loved them and washed (as it reads in some manuscripts) them from their sins by His own blood (Rev 1:5, 6). The leper living in the day of Christ had no hope in themselves or in their culture of being whole or clean. They were alienated from all social and spiritual life, crying as they went, "Unclean, unclean!" They could not approach the people of God, the temple of God, or find comfort outside of hoping for miraculous healing. But, Christ cleansed the lepers (Matt 8:3, Luke 5:13). That was the language and picture of what He does for every sinner. Even when it was their very conscience which was defiled, the blood of Christ removed that defilement. There is hope for the sexual sinner from the moral and psychological contamination. Again, the word used for washing by Paul speaks of a thorough cleansing, to be washed entirely from defilement. Paul experienced it himself and here gives it to all of us as an expression of our faith in Christ (Acts 22:16). The Christian is one that knows by experience this cleansing. The blood of Christ cleanses us from all sin (I John 1:7).

Second, the Christian is one that has gone from being unholy to being sanctified. "[Such] were some of you . . . , but ye are sanctified." They before worshiped not the God that they knew but chose to worship the creature, going on into many hurtful and sexual displays of creature worship (Rom 1:21–27). The idea presented by Paul though is that the Christian has been dedicated or consecrated toward a specific or holy end, set apart for something. This is the language of meaning and purpose that alone has value when it is unto God. The sinfulness of man, especially that which is expressed in sexual passions, exhibits that one is not after righteousness but after self-fulfillment and pleasure. Sexual desire expressed as identity is more apt than one realizes to letdown. It is an expression of what they are totally dedicated to, and that which cannot fulfill. There are none that are righteous. There are none that seek after God (Rom 3:10, 11). Instead, they are devotees to another god.

But this god that they devote themselves to can give them nothing. A common response to sex is what has been called postcoital dysphoria. This is the feeling of emptiness and sadness over the sexual encounter and dissatisfaction with the encounter itself is the earmark of this phenomenon. Amnon hated Tamar, who he once loved, the moment his lust was fulfilled (II Sam 13:1–15). Going back to the remarks of Peter, there is a promise of freedom and a buyer's remorse when the end is corruption (II Pet 2:19). Regardless of its etiology, postcoital dysphoria is prevalent. The build up to the sexual encounter promises more than it can deliver for one that has set their sense of fulfillment in that act. Sexual sins come with the baggage of a letdown when they are done. Solomon in chasing the strange woman said he mourned at last when his flesh and body were consumed. He cried over his foolish despising of true wisdom (Prov 5). The pleasure of sin is but for a season and gives no sense of greater fulfillment. So it is with all sin.

The chasing of the pleasure of sin is fleeting and results in a sense of waste. Even the most ardent hedonistic character like Oscar Wilde in the hour of death found no solace in his former days of pleasure seeking. There are no satisfied sinners. The worship of the creature creates chaos and not purpose. The worship of God alone can fulfill us and make us whole. As Augustine said, our heart is restless until it finds rest in God, the source of all beauty. We who are Christians were wasted but we are now sanctified. But the dead are in the house of lust (Prov 9:18).

Again, note the passive language of the monergistic work of God in salvation. We are set apart unto God. We are made unto Him. God now works out His righteousness in us. The old man that was corrupt we put off and have now put on the new man which is renewed in righteousness after the image of Christ (Eph. 4:22–24). There is now a lasting and real principle of goodness unto God that is being worked out in the believer. Where they were not right or good, now right and good are principles God is working in them. They could not give praise to God, now their lives resound with praise unto their God. As long as one lives in the foolishness of their own lusts, they are unholy. But when one is reconciled to God they can do true service as ministers of righteousness. "But God be thanked, that ye were the servants of sin, but ye have obeyed from the heart that form of doctrine which was delivered you. Being then made free from sin, ye became the servants of righteousness" (Rom 6:17, 18). Now they are holy unto their holy God.

Working back from the immediate change of being cleansed, and the radical change of being holy, we arrive at the fountainhead of the change. The Christian has gone from being lost to being saved, from being guilty before God to being justified before God. "[Such] were some of you . . . , but ye are justified . . . ." Sex that occurs outside of God's declared purposes and designs inevitably is laden with guilt, as all sin is; real guilt before the real Judge of all. Contemporary psychology may try to recouch that guilt and say that it is simply something that is self-imposed. But, no matter how we try to reshape our moral categories, sin, especially sexual sins, resurfaces in the experience of real guilt in our conscience. The sexual event ends with the moral evaluation that thunders our guilt before God. In John Bunyan's classic *The Holy Wars*, he told of the town of Mansoul under the sway of Diabolos, the character of the devil. In order to live in relative peace, the citizens cast Mr. Conscience into the lowest dungeon. But Mr. Conscience continued to cry out so loudly that it shook the very foundations of the town of Mansoul. There is a voice of real guilt that cannot be silenced in us. The conscience is the messenger of God written on our minds and hearts. Solomon said that it is the spirit of the Lord searching us inwardly (Prov 20:27). This is the greatest reason that mankind does not want to retain the thought of God in their minds (Rom 1:28).

The sinner who is trying to declare that sexual guilt is a social construct, a learned consequence of a repressive society, only attempts to skirt the reality of what one feels in the privacy of their own conscience. It is an act of wishful thinking. What we do sexually is not done in child-like innocence but in the moral context of absolute right and wrong and before a holy Judge that rightly adjudicates. That is a scary truth, but nonetheless true. They may press sexual categories on innocent children, but they anachronistically thrust those categories on them with Freudian zeal. They know that what they did was different from what a baby does when they are discovering and becoming aware of their physical members. They are aware that what they did was seen by God and contrary to God's commands and expressed will. And they know that they are guilty. They knew it would be so before they ever entered the act, choosing to do it anyway. Going about trying to unlearn guilty feelings with self-talk that one did nothing wrong is only further hardening one's heart in their sin against God.

Justification is a forensic or legal term. It brings up the real picture of our guilty soul before God. Some of you were fornicators and adulterers. Some of you were known before the court of God's justice in the most gross terms of your real sin and crimes against His holiness and righteousness. What could a liar and perjurer expect from the Judge who is the truth itself? They can only expect righteous judgment from God against them. This is the forensic reality of the evidence of our crimes being laid bare in the open court room of the Lord of all. But it can have a different end. Instead of the gavel coming down declaring our guilt and His righteous judgment, the gavel came down declaring us innocent of all. That is justification. You were guilty but you are justified, you are cleared of all charges. This is the heart of the Christian message. One can be guilty before God and yet be forensically declared of God to be not guilty. The basis of this is not God clearing the guilty. God will not clear the guilty because God is Just (Ex 34:7). There was one that declared Himself guilty in the stead of the sinner, Jesus Christ. Our sins were laid on Him, and He as the guilty one took the justice demanded on our guilt. He died the death that we earned instead of us. He stepped in the place of the sinner and thus allowed us to be justified before God. We stood before God with the righteousness of Christ and therefore are cleared (2 Cor 5:21).

This is the antithesis that lies behind the real context of right and wrong; the real categories of being unclean, unholy, and guilty. We stand before a righteous and holy God. We can try to ignore these realities and pretend as if they are not real. We can go about to appease our lusts, pretending that there are no evil and terrible consequences, presently and in the world to come. But, such foolishness will be short lived. It is a good thing for the Prodigal to see the real condition of his soul. It is a good thing for people to come to feel that there is no hope for them sitting on the fence and craving to be fed with the slop. As a sinner, they may repent and turn to their God. If they do, they will find themselves washed, sanctified, and justified before their God through Jesus Christ.

The Eschatology of Sex

Antithesis 5: That Which Ends in Heaven and That Which Ends in Hell

"But fornicators and adulterers God will judge . . . ." Hebrews 13:4

PART OF THE DENIAL of distinctions made by those who embrace egalitarian philosophies is the denial of anything beyond the present moment. John Lennon would ask us to imagine that there is no heaven or no hell below us, just what is here and now. Contemporary philosophers similarly contend that the thought of life enduring beyond death destroys meaning for the here and now, life coming to finality in finite time is said to be necessary to any sense of nominal purpose for life. Such an outlook may bolster a false sense of stoic bravery, staring starkly into oblivion without flinching, but this bleak outlook of nothing being beyond this world cannot bolster a thriving and living morality. If we live and die like dogs, then our mores are no different than the mores of a dog. Whether we snarl or wag our tails is a matter of ultimate indifference. The quality of one's life is judged by the direction and destination for which it aims. If we aim at nothing, we are morally bankrupt now and will be guilty in time to come.

There is an antithesis between this world and the world to come that was laid out before us by Christ. "And these shall go away into everlasting punishment: but the righteous into life eternal" (Matt 25:46). Suddenly, what we do here and now matters.

It has an end or purpose that will be realized then and not now. There is a need to set our eyes now on what will turn toward the best then and not the other way around. The atheist slogan that "there is probably no God, so you should enjoy yourself sexually right now" will hold little efficacy if they are wrong about their condition. Where this is all headed has tremendous bearing on what ought to be done right now.

Therefore, we must make eschatological distinctions in order to judge our conduct here and now. What we often forget about eschatology is that it is ethical and not esoteric. It is not about knowing exactly how future events unfold, as if we hold some sort of special knowledge, but rather knowing what ends are better to strive toward. We presently consider how this is shaped doctrinally from an eschatological point of view and then will consider axiology in the next antithesis. God declaring through His prophets what will be should always end in us asking the present question, what kind of person ought we to be now in the light of those declared ends (II Pet 3:11)? The declared ends of God are the goals to which He is infallibly aiming and directing all things. And His goals, by all sound ethical reasoning, ought to be ours. When Christ expounded on the last things, He highlighted a need for present watchfulness. This was brought to bear by the parable of the just and unjust servants, who both knew their Lord's instruction and his promise of coming again, going about their daily lives. One in the light of eschatology lived morally in watching over what was their Lord's. The other set aside eschatological truth and began to live unethically, contrary to the stated ends of their Lord. They became drunk and violent (Luke 12:42–48). Eschatology sets our priorities. That which is going to be speaks of what is important now. Eschatological truth will be brought to bear and that demands a present response.

We are warned in the Apocalypse that the wicked, under threat of final judgment, would not repent of their sexual immorality, among other things: "And the rest of the men . . . yet repented not of the works of their hands, that they should not worship devils, and idols of gold, and silver, and brass, and stone, and of wood: which neither can see, nor hear, nor walk: Neither repented they of their murders, nor of their sorceries, nor of their fornication, nor of their thefts" (Rev 9:20, 21). Thus, they showed the suitableness of their judgment. Going back to the declaration of Paul in regards to secular or hedonistic understanding of sex, Paul highlights the end of these things and there makes that eschatological end a reason to control one's sexual behavior. There, as was highlighted already, he spoke of those who keep the serving of the appetite as a chief end, as if the momentary self-fulfillment is all there is. "Meats for the belly, and the belly for meat . . . ." This is an enclosed ethical system that gives no thought to what will be. Paul corrects it eschatologically, "but God shall destroy both it and them" (I Cor 6:13). Those who live for the appetite, in other words, will find both themselves and that which they lust for destroyed. Their folly was rebuked by what will be, both the meat they look to satisfy their appetite and the appetite they seek to indulge will be brought to their eschatological end. They deny what will be and live instead for what will not be.

John agreed in a similar context that the world passes away and all its lusts. "Love not the world, neither the things that are in the world . . . . For all that is in the world, the lust of the flesh, and the lust of the eyes, and the pride of life, is not of the Father, but is of the world. And the world passeth away, and the lust thereof: but he that doeth the will of God abideth for ever" (I John 2–15–17). Do you see how eschatology is ethically relevant to the here and the now? Paul continued to replace their unsound and unethical sexual philosophy with a sound ethical philosophy, "Now the body is not for fornication, but for the Lord; and the Lord for the body." And that ethical philosophy is supported by our eschatological hope, "And God hath both raised up the Lord, and will also raise up us by his own power" (I Cor 6:13, 14). The end of our body is to be raised with its Lord.

God intends by His promise and in accordance with His power to bring us into a greater reality. As Christ taught, the present sexual reality we know will one day give way to a far better reality (Matt 22:29, 30). The power of God will change all of this.

Humanity will no longer need to continue by sexual means but will by the power of God enjoy endless life with God. We honor God's present purposes for sex and marriage, but we use it knowing that it is not our proper end.

The body matters and what we do in our body matters. It matters how it is used and to what ends. It matters because what we do in our bodies involves our worship now and is directed toward a greater end of worship hereafter. Paul taught that this body presently stands in weakness, in dishonor, in corruption, and in its naturalness (related to the physical world and its processes). But, just like the acorn, it is not intended to that end. There is a resurrection of this body. And, for those in Christ, it will be something greater. It will be in power, in honor, in incorruption, and spiritual (related to the invisible and spiritual realities yet to be realized, see I Cor 15:42–48). This is not a forsaking of the body here and now but a moral realization that it is intended by God to be something more and allowing what that is to set our priorities. The natural use of the body (that which is ordered by God and restrained by His commands) is good, how much more is His ends!

There is then an eschatology of the body, a purpose for a world to come beyond the now. Gnostic heresy denied purpose for the body for it dismissed it as evil and contrary to the nature of God. Adherents to Buddhism and Christian Science represent hardline examples of the extremes of this heresy. The message of salvation is offensive to gnostic sensibilities, that God would be incarnate, that God would live a life in the flesh, that God in that flesh would die for the sins of others, that He would be raised, and that He would thus live forever to intercede for those whom He saves. Christ was raised bodily and will forever abide thus with us. When He rose from the dead, He gave stress to the bodily nature. He invited them to handle Him and see that it was the very body that was crucified (John 20:27). He sat and ate with them to show that He was flesh and bones and not a spiritual manifestation (Luke 24:39–43). Gnostic reinterpretations forcing a docetic understanding (that Christ only appeared or seemed to have a body) cannot bear the weight of sound exegetical reading of the Scriptures. The apostles said they saw and touched Christ (I John 1:1).

The life that we live in this flesh now we live in hope and in the faith of the Son of God (I John 3:1–3). We work with our hands for His glory. We obey His commands for His glory. We enter marriages and raise children, instructing them in the nurture and commandments of the Lord, for His glory. This natural life of weakness is lived out in hope. The body then is important and what we do in the body is important. We will receive those things that are done in this body one day. Paul said, "Wherefore we labor, that, whether present or absent, we may be accepted of him. For we must all appear before the judgment seat of Christ; that everyone may receive the things done in his body, according to that he hath done, whether it be good or bad" (2 Cor 5:9, 10). There is a reward, a receiving back, yet to come. It will be individual to "everyone" or rather each one of us. It will be based on what we did "in" or "through" our bodies. It will be dispensed by Christ. And it will either be to a good end or an evil end to each individual. Paul in another place said that if we sow to the flesh we will get corruption back, but if we sow to the Spirit, we will get back life everlasting (Gal 6:6–9). Or as Daniel said about the doctrine of the resurrection, "And many of them that sleep in the dust of the earth shall awake, some to everlasting life, and some to shame and everlasting contempt" (Dan 12:2). This is what is set before us, the way of life and the way of death.

Paul indicated these two ends, good or evil, as the things that will be received back in accordance with the deeds we did with our bodies. Good or evil are adjectives in the accusative answering back to the things (also accusative) we receive. Good deeds receive good in return, so do evil deeds. The focus though is the things that will be. Paul follows the pattern of Christ in comparison of current physical (and even sexual) reality and the greater things of the resurrection. Again, in the answer of Christ to the Sadducees regarding marriage and childbearing in the world to come, He told them that they were in error due to their lack of knowledge of the Scriptures and that they were in error due to their lack of knowledge of the power of God (Matt 22:29). To the former error He cited the Word of God highlighting the present life of saints who have died. But, the latter error, regarding the power of God, He declared that God was to raise us up to a higher reality than this current physical reality, a reality comparable to the angels. Eyes have not seen and minds have not even begun to contemplate what God in His power has prepared for those that love Him (I Cor 2:9).

Paul connects this reality to the reward of the faithful who in repentance have turned from the evil sexual lusts and philosophies of this present evil world and the reward of the faithless who do not. He did so, as we already noted, with the Corinthians and also again with the Thessalonians. In the light of the coming of Christ and the resurrection, he encouraged them, "[This] is the will of God, even your sanctification, that ye should abstain from fornication: That every one of you should know how to possess his vessel in sanctification and honor; Not in the lust of concupiscence, even as the Gentiles which know not God . . . , because that the Lord is the avenger of all such, as we also have forewarned you and testified. For God hath not called us unto uncleanness, but unto holiness" (1 Thess 4:3–7). Note that God has ends which run contrary to sexual immorality. Note, also, that in the light of the goals of God, which find their end in the resurrection, that we strive to have self-control as we set ourselves apart unto God. And note that there is a warning of divine vengeance to any who do not hold to the ends determined by God by living in sexual uncleanness. Marriage is honorable, something worthy of being honored due to its undefiled nature, but sexual immorality will be judged (Heb 13:4). This dichotomy is prevalent. There is a fate for the righteous and the wicked. There is a fate where the filthy will be filthy still, and the just will be just still (Rev 22:11). They will irrevocably be what they are. Where the tree falls, there it stays (Ecc 11:3).

There is a good end to live for. When Paul told us that everything that happens does so for the good of those that love God, that good was the conforming of the believer to the image of Christ (Rom 8:28–30). The believer is putting on Christ now (Gal 3:27), but the end of this good is perfect sanctification (glorification) after the pattern of the resurrected Christ. Paul, when comparing the end of those whose god is their appetite,[1] said of the immoral that "[their] end is destruction," He laid this greater end before the believers, "For our conversation is in heaven; from whence also we look for the Savior, the Lord Jesus Christ: Who shall change our vile body, that it may be fashioned like unto his glorious body, according to the working whereby he is able even to subdue all things unto himself" (Phil 3:20, 21). In the context of purifying one's self in hope in this life, on the basis of the love of God, John also said, "Beloved, now are we the sons of God, and it doth not yet appear what we shall be: but we know that, when he shall appear, we shall be like him; for we shall see him as he is" (I John 3:2). What we are now and what we will be is related to what we do now. The Psalmist also described the joy and perfect fulfillment of awaking in the likeness of his Lord (Ps 17:15). This is, in context, a sanctifying truth that separated the psalmist from the wicked who live for the present life alone. Christ was raised to die no more (Rom.6:9). And we will eventually be like Him and forever be with Him. That is an end worth living for.

There is a greater good to live toward. We cannot live for the corruptible things when we were made to put on incorruption. This world is passing away with all of its lusts (I John 2:15-17). This body has a greater purpose of glorifying its Lord forever. For the Christian, this begins at conversion and never ends. There is a change coming in which we will be perfected toward that end. And that will be joy unspeakable (I Pet 1:3-9).

While the Christian lives for what will be, there are those who choose not to so live. The strange woman forgets the covenant of her God (Prov 2:16, 17). There are those who choose to set aside the ethics of eschatology and live as if the Lord delays His coming (Matt 24:48-50) or declare that there is nothing beyond this life for which we should live. There is a practical hedonistic philosophy that says that we ought to eat and drink now for tomorrow we will die (I Cor 15:32). The ethical eschatological view of the Scriptures

---

1. It is "belly" in the King James Version, and it is the same sexually immoral ones spoken of to the Corinthians.

stands as a stark warning. Peter said that all these things will be dissolved one day, and seeing that that is such, we should consider what kind of people we will be right now. Why? We should attach our ethic to our hope because we are looking for something far better, a new heaven and a new earth (a new physical reality) where righteousness dwells. How can we be counted now with those who walk according to their own lusts or rather their own ends (II Pet 3:1–14)? Paul agreed with this ethic when teaching about sexuality and our priorities that we set here in this world. He taught, "the time is short: it remaineth, that both they that have wives be as though they had none; And they that weep, as though they wept not; and they that rejoice, as though they rejoiced not; and they that buy, as though they possessed not; And they that use this world, as not abusing it: for the fashion of this world passeth away" (I Cor 7:29–31). It is not that we do not take those things seriously in this life. We ought to become fathers and mothers, husbands and wives, and in the teaching of the law to give instruction to the generation after us (Deut 6. Ps 78). He is not forbidding the proper use of these things here. We will need to weep. We will need to do business in the marketplace. We will need to use this world. But these things are not to be ends in themselves. It is the end of all things that justifies all our means.

The fact that what we do in our bodies now will matter forever is seen in the wrath of our Lord against those short-sighted souls who live for their lusts to be fulfilled now. Cursed are those who laugh now (Luke 6:25). Remember, our sins reveal our character. The sinful servant still called his absent Lord, "Lord" (Matt 24:48–50). But he went on living as if his Lord had no present Lordship, comforting himself with the doctrine of the Lord's delay. Men set their heart on evil when judgment is not deemed to be a present reality (Ecc 8:11). There is a Gnostic spirit in the nominal Christian world that claims a faith that has no practical place. The body can be indulged without any effect on what one is spiritually, is the refrain. But, what we do in the body here, continues there. "Appoint them their portion with the hypocrites" will be their righteous judgment (Matt 24:51)!

There is a place under judgment for those who are defined by their sin. Even if they call Christ Lord, the truth of their opposition is clearly seen by the unrepentant way in which they conducted their life. Again, see the subjects of God's wrath. "And the rest of the men which were not killed by these plagues yet repented not of the works of their hands . . . , Neither repented they of their murders, nor of their sorceries, nor of their fornication, nor of their thefts" (Rev 9:20, 21). Sexual sinners are part of these subjects of God's righteous wrath. These are they that have the wrath of God poured on them. It comes as no shock to the Christian that sexual sins are barriers to repentance. Sartre and Russell were not the first people to reject the idea of God due to a desire to indulge their sexual proclivities and they will not be the last. Paul included sexual sins among the reasons that men do not want to retain knowledge of God (Rom 1:26–28). And in the course of his treatise showed clearly the guilt that all have before God as subjects of His just wrath (Rom 3:16–20).

There is an order, a nature, which has been imposed on this world and all its inhabitants by its Lord. There is a cosmic rebellion at the heart of the sexual sinner (or any willing sinfulness). God created order. The natural use of the creature is found in the order imposed on the cosmos by its Lord. He created the cosmos freely from nothing. And He freely took its initial chaos brought into existence by His power and imposed His order or *telos* upon it in His wisdom. The order that exists in the world is His order. The imperatives that govern it are His commands that He has made known to mankind in history. His order and ends, as He has made known in time, are known to all. This is so, especially in the sexual aspects of His order. He created all things with a natural use. He gave the structure of marriage and family and communicated the will that mankind would multiply in that continuing framework. He since, in the unfolding of history, gave imperatives that supported that order and those ends.

The sexual sinner is in rebellion to all of this. They emerge from His order and try to return all things to chaos. They deconstruct His imperatives to the very foundations. Like the average penny-ante revolutionary, they go about destroying the existing order in order to create and impose an arbitrary order born in their own minds. They imagine their power and wisdom to be equal to or greater than their Lord. They believe they can unseat God from His throne, return all things to an initial chaos, and then in the absence of His Spirit moving on the waters, make something that is their own. They play gods trying to bring their own order to a fictitious chaos. There are consequences now to this foolishness (their lives never arise out of their self-imposed chaos) and there is an eternal consequence to this cosmic rebellion.

They have neither the wisdom of God nor the foundation of His eternal goodness to create anything, much less anything which can be the basis for a thriving societal structure. Like the house built on the sand, without being founded on the rock, its end is destruction (Matt 7:24–27). And, what is left but the cosmic rebel who tried to unseat their Lord. Marriage is honorable to the order imposed by the King of kings. Those who pursue sexual immorality will be judged (Heb 13:4). Note, then, the judgment that the Lord will bring and upon whom. Among other classes of sinners, the sexually immoral person will have their part in the lake of fire. "But the fearful, and unbelieving, and the abominable, and murderers, and whoremongers, and sorcerers, and idolaters, and all liars, shall have their part in the lake which burneth with fire and brimstone: which is the second death" (Rev. 21:8).

A word here of warning. The wrath of God is just and holy. It is rightly brought down on the head of the rebellious sinner. There is no one that reads or hears these words who has not been warned to flee from the wrath to come. As John warned the religious hypocrites, so now I warn the sexual sinner, flee from the wrath which is indeed coming (Matt 3:7). Flee into the arms of the one that can wash away all sin. I pray they will heed this warning. There is something yet to be said about our eschatological hope. However, it will be set aside as we ponder one more important antithesis. For now, I will leave this subject here in its antithesis.

The Axiology of Sex

Antithesis 6: That Which is Wise and That Which is Foolish

"For this is the will of God, even your sanctification, that ye should abstain from fornication: That every one of you should know how to possess his vessel in sanctification and honor . . . ."
First Thessalonians 4:3, 4

PAUL REASONED WITH FELIX about self-control (Acts 24:25). He reasoned with a head of state about this very subject matter (i.e., sexuality), much like John the Baptist did with the king (Matt 14:3). The Christian is right to raise this matter as a political and societal standard for the good and blessing of any state. Paul also reasoned thus with the church (I Thess 4:3, 4). There is not a different standard for those in or outside of the church for all stand before the judgment of God. On the heels of considering the end of this matter, it is necessary to step back and consider the question of ultimate value, Axiology. Since there is a way that seems happy for now but ultimately leads to destruction, is that way of any true and present value (Matt 7:13, 14)? What profit is there to enjoy the pleasure of sin for this season in exchange for the eternal loss of one's soul, or the political deterioration of our state, or the ecclesiastical corruption of our fellowship and ministry (Mark 8:36). This is the same consideration given for our contemplation by Christ, "And when he had called the people unto him with his disciples also, he said unto them, Whosoever will come after me, let him deny himself, and take up his cross, and follow me. For whosoever will save his life shall lose it; but whosoever shall lose his life for my sake and the gospel's, the same shall save it" (Mark 8:34, 35). Where does the value lie? Does it lie in unfettered self-indulgence or in a denial of self?

The scriptural estimation of value is very different than the anthropocentric (human-centered) or rather egocentric (individual-centered) system of values that govern culture. Once the truth that there is one Lord and God over all, the distinction between Creator and creature, is jettisoned there is nothing left but a myriad of individual things without unity, without meaning, without purpose, without destiny, and therefore without value. Everything is self-contained in its own space/time without the absoluteness of God to relate them. The sad truth of the individualistic culture, despite its leap of faith in saying all is one, is that each individual is alone, isolated, without anything to relate it to another. Unifying concepts are divinely given truths that make no sense in a world without God, and philosophers grope blindly after them in their studies. But they cannot be grasped unless they first revere their God (Prov 1:7, 9:10).

The world that the Lord God created and reigns over is the only world where value has meaning. Saying that this is of greater or lesser value than that, or this ought to be, or that thing is better all assumes the reality of meaning and worth, as well as a standard by which real judgment can be made. God alone sits as the maker and evaluator of all things. Without Him there is no value. God is the foundation of all true axiological statements. And if we are to make moral and aesthetic judgments about sexual values, we begin with God as Lord, as we do with all other things.

The contention in discussing values in our contemporary culture remains at this starting point. Unless one arrives at something that has intrinsic value, that which is worthy in and of itself, then all discussion of value is relative. If all value remains at the level of the extrinsic, that is, the value of a thing being found in something outside of itself, as a means to something else, then nothing has any lasting and unchanging value. The inability of autonomous human philosophy to provide a unifying concept of the Good, and its practical relationship to this world, has caused all discussion of axiological musing to turn to the shifting sands of human and cultural tastes and opinions. The most hideous thing can be preferred by someone and therefore declared to have some sort of value. The psychologist will describe why a certain individual is drawn to this thing or that. The sociologist or economist will try to explain why this trend or that waxes or wanes in a fickle society. But we are left with no sense of real value, only shifting desires and motives for why some certain thing at some certain time is deemed to have value; even if we intuitively know that such a thing is rubbish.

The Christian has a different starting point. We begin with the God of whom the angels sing, "Holy, Holy, Holy" (Isa 6:1, 2). We ascribe glory to this God. We say of His Son that He is worthy (Rev 4, 5). And this Good, unlike Plato's good, has a real relationship to this world as its Creator and Lord. He is the Most-High God upon which all intrinsic value and all other values can be weighed. On the basis of God and the revelation of Himself alone, we can begin to speak of things being better, greater, sweeter, and of more value in this ever-changing world because all things are related to Him and more or less are conformed to His expressed will.

The high-mindedness of man has set themselves up as the source of values, as if man was worthy and all other things find their value only in relation to their worth. By this foolishness they reduce God to the level of the extrinsic. There is, among some contemporary philosophers, a debate about the axiological question of God's existence. That is, the argument concerning what value-impact a belief in God has for mankind as a whole or for the individual in particular. Even the argument of those who favor God act as if the question is whether or not God adds value to human life, whose value in their minds is paramount. The prosperity gospel proponents would find a home with such a philosophy. They would find value in God as He granted their desires but find no value in a God that ordained tribulation to them for His own glory. They would reject that kind of God. The adversary of God would reject God on the same basis, that God added no value to their lives. A God restraining them from their desires, judging their sin, and giving them a portion of sorrows to endure was not a worthy God from their perspective. They will not say with Paul that the suffering now experienced is not worthy to be compared to the glory which shall be revealed (Rom 8:18). God is worthy regardless of what petty value-impact we think we are worthy of expecting. Men love darkness but God is light without darkness (John 3:19, I John 1:5). He is greater, He is the Most-High God. He dwells in the light that no man can approach (I Tim 6:16).

Also, the determination of true value can never rise any higher than the fidelity of its estimator. Modern axiological studies describe what fallible men desire as they change. But who are these fickle estimators? It is said of them that there are none of them that are good (Rom 3:10–12). Their mouths are full of deception (Rom 3:13, 15). Can we trust the marketplace of deceitful merchants to tell us the true quality and worth of their wares? Our government provides currency which they say has value. As long as there is trust in their authority then that currency holds some value to us. But what do we find them to be? They are broken reeds that cannot hold the weight of our trust. They manipulate and inflate that currency for their own gain, robbing and oppressing the poor. We often feel the eroding of that trust as we do business in their economy. Unless there is revelation from the one that is worthy of our trust to give value to extrinsic things, then all statements of value are wavering and uncertain. Our God cannot lie, He is the God of truth (Num 23:19, Titus 1:2, Heb 6:18, Deut 32:4).

When all values of mankind remain extrinsic, things have value only as a means to something else. Eventually and even inevitably the relative value of those things sought will lose their savor. The lack of the truly intrinsic, reduces all to hedonism. The end of all things is the pleasure of the consumer. All things are consumable and once consumed are of no more value than the rind of the fruit. They may be dressed up with the rhetoric of the qualitative hedonist, the epicurean seeking of higher pleasures (e.g., health, friendship, etc.). But those things being extrinsic alone are empty and destined to slip through our fingers like sand and be reduced to ash as the grave diggers cover us over. The intrinsic worth of the eternal God who gives good gifts is the basis for knowing the value of the things in this world and our choices regarding those things (James 1:17). This is especially true since the advent of sin. If all is extrinsic, then all that pleases the individual becomes relatively valuable and as long as they have relative value to man, they seem good. However, there are things we know should not be chosen for God has revealed His displeasure with them. There are things that God rejoices in and things that are a stench, an abomination, to Him. There are things He declared to be good and things He declared evil, repugnant, and hurtful.

That is the understanding of biblical Axiology. The value of all things are related to God, His expressed will, and His judgment of all things. We are never the final arbiters of values. That which is highly esteemed by man is too often little esteemed by God (Luke 16:15). He sees as we do not see and knows as we know not. That which we believe holds value over time rarely does. Even the things we believe to be worthy of our strength, time, and investment are vanity, as Solomon in all his wisdom learned (See Ecclesiastes). The Most-High God created, evaluated (saw), and ascribed goodness and value to the things He created (called them good). In the process of creating, He created man. And recognizing a value lacking in His work, He created woman for man. Human sexuality was the product of God evaluating and creating that which was valuable in the context of man. He also ordained a structure for human sexuality, a worthy cause for man to leave all and cling to, a one flesh union of a man to his own wife. Behind the backdrop of this, is a mandate to have children and fill the earth, taking dominion and bringing all its potential under man's utility. That came from God's declaration. That is the value, the surpassing value that God ascribed to human sexuality. "For thus saith the Lord that created the heavens; God himself that formed the earth and made it; he hath established it, he created it not in vain, he formed it to be inhabited: I am the Lord; and there is none else" (Isa 45:18).

The curse of sin brought a reality to human sexuality that is not good or valuable. There was the psychological reality of shame that entered into it. They went from being naked without shame to being ashamed of their nakedness (compare Gen 2:25 with 3:7). There is the advent of sorrow in the bearing of children, no doubt including the loss of potential through sin brought to the joyous dominion mandate (Gen 3:16). There is the struggle of authority that sin brought to the husband-and-wife relationship, built on the breach of trust brought in by sin (Gen 3:16). By the end of the fourth chapter of Genesis, sinful lust corrupted the very ordinance of marriage through the perverseness of polygamy (Gen 4:19). Sin brought the reality that there are aspects of sexuality that should not be sought, they have no value to man, only potential harm. And, as we already saw, potential judgment.

But there yet remains aspects of sexuality that have great value. Christ highlighted that from the beginning the original value is still there, that man can still go about leaving all and cling-ing to it (Matt 19:4–6). Again, marriage is honorable with respect to all. The sexual activity that occurs in the marriage bed is without any defilement (Heb 13:4). That word honor is *timios*. That term has a recognition of value and preciousness embedded in it. It is seen as a worthy end to pursue. And, most importantly, God sees it as worthy of honor. It has the functional value of bringing life and fulfillment of God's mandate to fill the earth. Thus, God blesses it (Ps. 127, 128). It has aesthetic value for its wonder and delight (Prov 30:18, 19). It has moral value in that it is free from sin and its defilement (Heb 13:4).

Nowhere is this principle of value more clearly seen, as it relates to sexuality, than in the first part of the book of Proverbs. Wisdom is compared to folly as a prevailing theme of the first nine chapters. Knowledge is knowing what, and wisdom is knowing how to use that knowledge for the good. Wisdom is an exercise of seeking the greater value, discretion is wisdom rejecting that which is of lesser value. Wisdom itself is of greater value than folly for it is that which comes from God that enables us to choose those things which have the greatest value-impact in our lives and which most honors our Lord.

The first nine chapters of Proverbs present the call of Lady Wisdom in contrast to the call of Madame Folly. Lady Wisdom offers life, while Madame Folly offers momentary pleasure that leads to death. Wisdom offers sure and valuable ends, while Folly offers only instability, uncertainty, and regret. To hearken to the voice of Wisdom is to be preferred to giving ear to the wooing of Folly who slays troops of strong men by her guile. While the greater warning is against idolatry, the call of wisdom toward life and the call of folly toward death surround the theme of sexual morality. It presents the value of a man rejoicing with the wife of his youth versus the call of adulterous lust which destroys the very soul. And the father urges the son to have wisdom in this matter, for it has a surpassing value and out of it is all good in life issuing forth.

Paul has a similar call to wisdom when he wrote to the Thessalonians. He urged them, as the father in Proverbs, to sanctify themselves to God in abstaining from sexual immorality (I Thess 4:3). He proclaimed this to be God's will for us, which is to be sought over our own will, after the pattern of our Lord (Ps 40:8). God's will is for you to be His, for His use. That is our sanctification, at least in a non-salvific understanding of sanctification. Sexual immorality is the forgetting of the covenant of our God (Prov 2:17) to serve our own lust. To sanctify ourselves to Him means that we must seek to abstain from, or more strictly to hold ourselves away from, this sin. The will of God and your sanctification are appositional realities. The abstaining is inseparable from this sanctification.

Now, how can we exercise this abstention? The answer to how is wisdom, the knowing how; "That every one of you should know how to possess his vessel in sanctification and honor, not in the lust of concupiscence, even as the Gentiles which know not God" (I Thess 4:4, 5). A pair of infinitives bridge the understanding of what we know and the bodily world in which we act; we are to know and to control. This self-control is contrary to contemporary wisdom that tells men to perform their innermost desires publicly. The voice of folly calls this authenticity, but it is the destruction of any valuable authenticity, a display of utter weakness of character and not true strength. "He that hath no rule over his own spirit is like a city that is broken down, and without walls" (Prov 25:28). It is not an authentic or genuine city if it is sacked and burned. Folly leaves broken and defenseless people, unable to protect others and unable to defend themselves. Strength is control, strength is truly authentic.

Here then we see the value of biblical wisdom. We have this vessel, this body and soul that is meant to exist for the glory of God (See I Sam 21:5). There are many that take the term vessel, as used by Paul to the Thessalonians, as a Hebrew idiom to mean wife instead of body. While it was used so by Peter, it was not so used by Paul (I Pet 3:7). There is, to the contrary, a broader point of the need for self-control beyond the sexual (not defrauding one's brother, I Thess 4:6), which makes the use of wife as vessel, instead of body, lack interpreting power in context. The lust of this world calls on us to take that vessel of our body and use it for that which is opposed to its Lord, to spoil and defile it from its purpose. The voice of wisdom gives us knowledge to see and understand the truth of God concerning all of this. And it transforms that knowledge into an ability to do the will of God. Grace through faith is the means of saving and sanctifying the one who believes. The Psalmist would have fainted, if he did not believe to see (Ps 27:13, 14).

The second infinitive, *ktaomai*, is translated well by the King James Version as possess. It speaks of holding something under one's own authority. It is value kept or saved or treasured up as opposed to being squandered and wasted like the Prodigal's riches. We have acquired the treasure of our Lord's presence in these earthen vessels (II Cor 4:7), and, knowing the surpassing value of that, we keep these vessels for Him. This is a call to patient endurance, to a virtuous life of self-control, by the grace of God. "In your patience possess ye your souls" (Luke 21:19). This vessel is easily broken and only has value in the will of the one who owns it. As long as we keep ourselves, we maintain the value His will has given. For Christ we work to bring our bodies in subjection to His will. Paul said, "I keep under my body, and bring it into subjection:

lest that by any means, when I have preached to others, I myself should be a castaway" (I Cor 9:27).

These extrinsic values of self-control and integrity, especially in the restraint from sexually immoral behavior, run opposite to a culture that praises the narcissistic and histrionic exhibitions of the sexually depraved. To value things as God values them and to bear that out in the consistent choices you make in life is what can rightly be called godliness and piety. Such a life is a life of integrity and wisdom. God has given you a sexual nature and sexual desires for a purpose. There is value right there. There is the evaluation of His created order in you that causes Him to say that this is very good. What is that purpose? Is that purpose for you to go about as if that purpose was not real? Is it for you to give into every passing desire that is not in line with God's evaluation? Of course, it is not, that would be an absurdity. Your purpose given to you by God is to prepare to be a husband and a father (or, if female, to be wife and a mother), and to perpetuate that into the future by preparing the next generation to do the same. Therein lies the value of sexuality. Regardless of how the world teaches us to covet evil, there is value in pursuing His order. It is better. And wisdom, the know-how of all this, is greater than all folly. It involves self-control as you pursue the treasure of God's will instead of the folly of your own. And in the pursuit of that order, if God does not bring you into those ends, He will yet be honored by your life. Striving after godliness is a life informed by true value.

This requires us to be willing at all times to set aside that which is not good and to be thoroughly informed by God as to what is and is not of value. It also requires us to be circumspect as to possible dangers. We should not delay marriage for other supposed goals, if we are finding ourselves struggling to contain our lusts, for it is better to marry (I Cor 7:1–9). We should in marriage be mindful of one another that there be fulfillment without wandering temptation (*ibid*). All of this highlights the knowledge of wisdom in the realm of our sexuality. The ability of judgment between right and wrong, value and worthlessness, safety and danger, is the outworking of the image of our God in us. This is godliness in sexuality.

Our exercise in Axiology goes beyond this world and this life. We are laying up value or treasure toward something greater. Paul saw the value of that reality as being far better (Phil 1:23). Thus, Paul, when teaching specifically about the matter of sexuality, reminded us of the greater end of which we already spoke in our discussion of eschatology. He reminded us that those who have wives will be as though they had them not (I Cor 7:29). Our happiness or blessedness is not contained in those things apart from our greater hope. The value of that world to come is what gives value to the world that now is. A self-contained pursuit of happiness apart from a greater hope is of no lasting value, it fades as a flower. And for many, the treasure they lay up is wrath and cursing and not blessedness.

Christ spoke of a blessedness that is a present reality (blessed are those now) as we give ourselves to His greater ends (Matt 5:3–12). When we have a character that commits to His glory (being poor in spirit, being merciful, hungering and thirsting after His righteousness, etc.), then we have the reality of blessedness now and glorious promises of greater things as dividends. In this vein of thought, marriage is presently worthy of honor in God's eyes and is set as a foil to the future judgment of those who defile it (Heb 13:4). Christ said, "Lay not up for yourselves treasures upon earth, where moth and rust doth corrupt, and where thieves break through and steal: But lay up for yourselves treasures in heaven, where neither moth nor rust doth corrupt, and where thieves do not break through nor steal: For where your treasure is, there will your heart be also" (Matt 6:19–21).

Part 2

Sex in Terms of Synthesis

Introduction to Part 2

"He hath made every thing beautiful in his time: also he hath set the world [eternity] in their heart, so that no man can find out the work that God maketh from the beginning to the end."
Ecclesiastes 3:11

GOD HAS SET IN the hearts of all desire for peace and wholeness, for unity and understanding, which can only be provided by God. In our above commentary, a certain tension, though a necessary one, has been declared. Sex as viewed from the terms of antithesis emphasizing the abandoned truths of the transcendent God, mankind as created by Him, God's holy law, the state of the lost before a just God, the frightening reality of final judgment, and the need of present sacrifice and self-control in striving toward greater ends. The tensions that are created are real and impactful. It forces each of us to see ourselves in the light of God's truth, the antitheses. Are we, in that light, guilty or innocent, are we honorable or shamed, are we wise or foolish, are we in a state of victory or a state of defeat, are we by grace made fit for heaven or by justice made fit for hell? This tends toward a state of dissonance where we either excuse ourselves to think ourselves on the right side of the antitheses or rather allow an honest assessment of our lives. I pray that each reader opts for the latter, as painful as it may be.

To leave this subject there is to fail to see a greater reality. This reality is not antithesis but synthesis, or rather unity. There is unity provided to us by God as a common gift of His grace to humanity (marriage) and unity we find with God by a special work of His grace to the redeemed (reconciliation). There is a wholeness that needs to be brought to the forefront of our thoughts. This unity, though, is not a false one that ignores the real antitheses that have been declared. Jungian psychology falsely declared that wholeness could be had by ignoring or denying that the antitheses of God are so. By embracing a false unity, he ignored the reality of good and evil, God and creation, and so on. This did not result in wholeness or health, but it brought about a deeper psychosis and an even more shattered psyche. Those who embrace a false unity are doomed to be further fractured by their sin. Again, those that will not build on the rock are doomed to a great fall (Matt 7:24–27).

The Teleology of Sex
Synthesis 1: From Singleness to Unity

"It is not good for man to be alone. . . . And they two shall be one flesh." Genesis 2:18, 24

GOD ALONE CAN PROVIDE true synthesis. And He has done so in this world, as it relates to this matter of sexuality. There is a place of unity provided to mankind by the common grace of God. God is said to make two (antithesis) to be one (synthesis or unity). It is something God does, He joins two together. These are the words of Christ that describe marriage, "Wherefore they are no more twain, but one flesh. What therefore God hath joined together, let not man put asunder" (Matt 19:6). This truth, as has already been seen, begins with absolute antithesis. There is the antithesis of Creator and creature. God in the beginning created. And then there is the antithesis which God immediately brought forth, male and female (Matt 19:4). And the antitheses continue to unfold; man/wife and father/mother. But, in this there is a unity provided by God to mankind. And this is the setting for the unity God brought into reality by His grace. Christ quotes the text of Genesis, "For this cause shall a man leave father and mother, and shall cleave to his wife: and they twain shall be one flesh" (Matt 19:5). God made a means for the man who was alone to find wholeness and unity with another. All of this is worth unpacking in order to see the amazing value (the axiological reality) of marriage. It is a honorable or precious gift given to us.

First, consider the man alone in isolation. God brought forth in creation a reality outside or apart from Himself. He ordered that reality by asserting antithesis, dividing this thing from that thing. But, when man was created, man was initially created alone. The only reasoning revealed regarding the intent of God in creating divisions is here in making man alone and then showing the need for there to be two prior to creating the second. In other words, here God desired for man to know His reason for antithesis within mankind prior to actualizing it. We have no such deliberation about why God separated land from sea or among any of the variety of living things. No such division initially for man existed, not because God was Himself ignorant of what man needed, but as an early theology of grace to be brought forth. Man was made to see all the divisions and distinctions that existed in this world and how those things allow for the perpetuation of life. And man was allowed by God to see that there was no helper along his side in this life. In that realization of man, brought by the revelation of God to him, it was declared by God for the first time that there was something in His creation that was not good, man dwelling alone (Gen 2:18).

Isolation is one of the stinging realities of this fallen world. The heart knows its own bitterness, and strangers cannot enter into its joy (Prov 14:10). The worse punishment one can endure is solitary confinement. The theme of isolation and loneliness makes up a vast majority of artistic expression as it tries to deal with common human experience. In the garden man could, under the order of his God, reason about God's creation, categorize it, and name it. And there in the exercise of coming to know and understand the world that God made, with God as his teacher, man came to know this pain, "there was not found any help meet [i.e., suitable] for him" (Gen 2:20). Man was alone in the physical world and God encouraged him to see that truth. God said, "It is not good that the man should be alone; I will make him an help meet for him" (Gen 2:18). And who did He say this to? He said it to man. He said it to man before He showed man all the glory of His created order and asked man to reason about and categorize it. "You are alone, and what you need, I will create for you!" This is a foreshadowing of what God would say to sinful man, doing what they could not do for themselves, that by grace He would provide for them all that was needed to save them (Jer 31:31–34, Heb 8).

The thesis became the antithesis. God created them male and female. There is not the narcissistic mirror image of male and male, but something now also human that is distinctly different from the male. There was now two, *arsen* (the Greek for male related to the term strength) and *thélus* (the Greek word for female related to the term of nurturing breast). Moses described the creation of the woman as an act of grace to man, where man passively from a deep sleep had God take from his side that which would be the woman (Gen 2:21, 22). She was indelibly related to man, bone from his bones and flesh from his flesh (Gen 2:23). Paul would recount the priority: the woman was first of the man (I Cor 11:12), the woman was for the man (I Cor 11;9), and, again, man was first created and then the woman (I Tim 2:13). The woman was the first experience of grace given to man after creation and all initial blessings seem to flow from that intended unity. God provided that which man lacked, a suitable or compatible help or partner in life to aid man in his commission. Wholeness came from God.

Man, then, was in the state of synthesis, having that which was related to and suitable to him in the world created and governed by his God. So, God guided man from thesis to antithesis to synthesis. In this world God provided existential fulfillment for man in uniting him to the woman in marriage. The good that was absent in man being alone was fulfilled by a man being united to his wife. God brought man from being alone to being one. Christ, quoting Adam as a prophet of God revealing the word of God, quoted the Scriptures, "Therefore shall a man leave his father and his mother, and shall cleave unto his wife: and they shall be one flesh" (Gen 2:24, Matt 19:5). This was no small blessing of wholeness but was applicable in the days of Christ and to us under His Lordship 6,000 years later. It was meant for all the human race in continuance.

Adam was the first prophet of God giving the first prophetic utterance of man recorded in history in that which Christ quoted above. Christ the Son who is the final voice from God took up the truth of that first prophetic utterance. Christ honored the word of God first given to man that proclaimed the wonder of the covenantal union of a man and his wife and set it forth to yet be the perpetual reality of blessedness for mankind. A man would leave the mother and father that produced him and seek and unite to his own wife, and those two will also become one. The oneness of covenantal faithfulness and covenantal love is seen in the leaving all to cleave unto. The tie of familial bonds a man has to his kindred is not to be compared to the bond he now enters with his wife. What is said of them can be said of no other relationship, they are one. They are, according to Barnes, "one in law, in feeling, in interest, in affection. They shall no longer have separate interests, but shall act in all things as if they were one - animated by one soul and one wish . . . ."[1] Man gains a true fellow in this life when he gains a wife. And all that is done by the mother and father appears to be preparatory to this wonderful end.

It was the first man and first woman together that were made by God and joined together by God that received the commission of God to go forward and be fruitful (Gen 1:27, 28). The language of Adam's prophecy is the means by which the dominion mandate is to be carried out; men and women, becoming husbands and wives, becoming fathers and mothers. From this, mankind as a whole would fill the earth and subdue it. Children would come from them sharing a mixture of both their traits in one and looking to them to guide them in the same path in the way of the Lord. They as one would be honored together under the law and, as will yet be seen, become the model of eternal fellowship in a microcosm.

Of importance in the mind of God, as a gift of grace, is what they mean in this life one to another. The commentary of Moses after the words of Adam were this, "And they were both naked, the man and his wife, and were not ashamed" (Gen 2:25). This

---

1. Barnes, Albert (1834); Notes on the Bible. From note on Matthew 19:5.

not only describes a state of innocence prior to the advent of sin, but the truth of marital intimacy that even yet transcends the fall. It was as man and wife that they were naked. And it was as man and wife that they were without shame in that state. Marriage is honorable and the bed is without defilement (Heb 13:4). Certainly, something of this was lost to them in the fall, as they hid from God in their sin because of their nakedness. They became ashamed before God. But Christ does not diminish the present reality of this. The fact that God joined them and the fact that a man and wife are yet perpetually one flesh, means that this is yet a blessing of marriage, especially godly marriage. They can come together as one without shame. They can in mutual love be able to have perfect knowledge of one another without any division or any hiding one from another. They can in good conscience and without shame be themselves without fear before the other. They can enjoy one another and help one another in the most intimate of ways; there being no fear of rejection in the faithfulness and love of godly marriage. Paul even states that they can and should minister to one another for mutual help and encouragement in such an intimate way (I Cor 7:3–5). This can never be the innocent, safe, loving, and intimate reality in the chaos of sexual sin. This love bears all and endures all, it never fails (I Cor 13).

Christ addressed the permanence of this covenantal love. "Wherefore they are no more twain, but one flesh" (Matt 19:6). Early Syriac and Ethiopic translations say they are one body. To this agreed Paul when he said that a man ought to love his wife as his own body, a thing he nourishes, and calls the man to be the savior of the body (Eph 5:23, 28, 29). They are "no more" two. They are permanently one. God has "joined together" into one flesh the man and woman. They are yoked together like oxen or a team of horses. They go forward together, inseparable in their progress, sharing with one another everything on the journey. They rest together, they work together, they enjoy the fruit of their work together. This is intended by God to be without end in this world. The man by an act of covenant cleaves to his wife, and God as Lord in the same act unites them. The permanency view of marriage is just that, as long as the spouse lives, they are united in covenant (Rom 7:2, I Cor 7:39). This is the basis of our culture's traditional vow, "till death parts us!"

This one flesh unity goes deeper than the purpose of procreation. This intimacy speaks of a purpose of producing delight and the mutual pleasure they have in one another. The Shunamite delighted in Solomon and Solomon in the Shunamite (Song of Solomon). This is a mutual ministry of husband to wife and wife to husband, as well as a mutual ownership and right to one another (I Cor 7:3–5). Solomon called upon his children[2] to find physical satisfaction in their spouse alone, to delight unto ecstasy in their love (Prov 5:15–19). Here the marriage bed is described as being an honorable and undefiled place of sanctified pleasure (Heb 13:4). Again, this is so for both man and wife as ministering one to another. The one flesh unity also speaks of intimacy of fellowship that is deepened in the experience of sexual intercourse. Adam "knew" his wife and by that act of intercourse, or knowing, God gave them a child (Gen 4:1). The Hebrew word *yada* often is used for intimacy of fellowship and even for entering into a relational covenant with another (Gen 18:19, God knew or chose Abraham). The sexual act in marriage is a repeated reenactment of that covenant. And it continuously ministers a sense of closeness to one's spouse. Sex appears to be physically designed for humanity to know one another, for the male and female to have such intimacy of knowledge. The human being is the only mammal that has the capacity of a face-to-face encounter in their physical relationship. Biblical marriage involves the man and wife knowing each another. And all of this produces a shared interest for the man and wife to have together. Peter declares that they are heirs together of life (I Pet 3:7). Their eternal interests are forever united by their one flesh relationship. This is so much the case that the apostles encouraged the believing spouse, who found themselves in the unfortunate position of having a marriage with an unsaved spouse, that their relationship sanctifies the other and gives great

2. Or as Solomon was instructed by David his father, depending on where one sees the instruction of David coming to an end, which started in Prov 4:1.

hope that the unbelieving spouse will be won to the Lord (I Pet 3:1, 2, I Cor 7:13, 14).

After the joining, they are not to be seen anymore as two. This is a holy place of God's work and not to be defiled. The warning of Christ to mankind is to respect this divinely given institution. "What therefore God hath joined together, let not man put asunder" (Matt 19:6). Do not seek on a personal level to diminish this union. Do not enter it lightly, but soberly. Do not be lax in working to maintain it in love. Do not let unfaithful eyes wander to something else (Matt 5:28). Do not seek to diminish it on a societal level. Do not rearrange its parameters or redefine its meaning. Do not disregard it as important. Do not allow it to be dissolved without legal, or rather biblical, cause.

The context of all the words of Christ are concerning the question of divorce. God hates divorce (Mal 2:16). Sin is the reality that seeks to destroy marriage. God, Christ, in mercy to the one sinned against allows exceptions to His general rule on divorce, sexual immorality and abandonment (Matt 19:9, I Cor 7:15). But even here there should not be a quick rush on the part of the wronged party to allow its dissolution. God sought reconciliation with adulterous Israel (Hos 2 & 3, Ezek 16). Setting aside God's merciful exceptions, mankind sins by allowing marriage to be so easily dissolved. One of the great harms of our own society was the advent of no-fault divorce and its removal of all civil and legal liability for the breaking of the marriage covenant; a covenant which has far reaching consequences on any society. No-fault divorce has done more harm to the generations than can be counted, more than any other attack on the marriage institution. It is blasphemy to contradict God, to treat as common what God has highly valued. What is adultery but a sin against the unity that God authored between two. What is divorce but a despising of that unity. What is fornication but a declaration that one does not desire God's unity and seeks to find wholeness outside of God and His expressed will.

Blessings to mankind flow from this unity. In the one flesh unity of marriage masculinity finds the fullness of its flourishing. The man finds honor in leadership, self-sacrifice, and a worthy cause for his courage and endurance to be displayed. He there has a tangible cause to maintain by integrity and faithfulness. Femininity flourishes here as well. There, in the home, the woman wisely builds, faithfully nourishes, and with moral strength and beauty shows Christ to generations. There is no other setting for both masculinity and femininity to find the fulness of its flourishing.

The work of the man and wife together is codified in God's law. The honor of both father and mother is written forever on the stone tablets by the very finger of God (Exo 20:12). There is no Corban rule or tradition that can relieve any responsibility to honor and care for both (Matt 15:4–6). Jesus modeled this even in the hour of His death as He cared for the needs of His mother (John 19:26). It is faithfulness that provides for one's own (I Tim 5:8). It is right for children to obey their parents and in doing so they bear the promise of blessings in this life (Eph 6:1–3). Children inherit the blessings of their fathers (Prov 19:14). And all throughout the Proverbs, it is the child that obeys and honors their parents that inherited such blessings.

Protecting such a cherished unity in this world is a mandate for any government. And there is no unity more despised by those who hate their Creator. It is a unity also treasured by the church. When choosing out and judging the men who take leadership in the church, they are to seek those who, among other qualifications, are the husband of one wife (I Tim 3:2). While some limit such a quality to a compliance check of whether one has been divorced and remarried, such a legalistic interpretation misses the point of the qualification. Surely such a qualification does address polygamy and the church should be able to judge on its basis whether or not any man had biblical grounds for any divorce and subsequent remarriage (which judgment few churches are willing to exercise). But that still misses the point. Any leader in the church must be a faithful husband, devoted to the covenant relationship God gave to him. Any man who is not a devoted husband (unless providence has not afforded him a wife), showing due benevolence and honor to his wife, then such a one is unfit to lead in the church. The one flesh union should be modeled in the church by its leadership, so that all may see and know what it looks like and aspire to have it. A husband that is harsh or absent is just as unqualified to lead as one who has taken a second wife. But sadly, pulpits are filled with men who forsake their home due to them meeting some arbitrary and legalistic item on a compliance checklist.

That modeling passes on to how a man cares for the fruit of that one flesh relationship. A man who does not model fatherhood is equally unfit to lead in a church. The one flesh union of man and wife gives cohesion to the lives of the children that are so raised. The wise wife will ensure the care of the needs of the children (Titus 2:4, 5). The husband provides compassionate nourishment and loving discipline. This is to be modeled by the lives of church leaders. "[A bishop must be] one that ruleth well his own house, having his children in subjection with all gravity; (For if a man know not how to rule his own house, how shall he take care of the church of God?) . . . (I Tim 3:1–5)." This was a quality God Himself looked for in the faith of Abraham. "For I know him, that he will command his children and his household after him, and they shall keep the way of the LORD, to do justice and judgment; that the LORD may bring upon Abraham that which he hath spoken of him" (Gen 18:19). It is the chief role of the father to bring the children up, to nurture them, and to guide them (Eph 6:4). A father that forsakes this role is unfit because his life bears the mark of one that denies the faith (I Tim 5:8).

The idea of the ruling of the husband is a stumbling block to our culture, but it embraces the role of caring for the family. To rule is to care for. This is not a despotic domineering like character being called for. Many men have or should have been disqualified from ministry due to their unkind, cruel, selfish, and mean spirited parenting styles. They are those who provoke their children to wrath (Eph 6:4). That is the opposite of this caring rule. What does it then mean to rule one's house? The word is often translated as managing, leading, or maintaining (Rom 12:8, I Thess 5:12, I Tim 5:17, Titus 3:8, 14). It is a compound word meaning "to stand before." This carries many different connotations. They stand before in the sense of protecting, going before them in the way, or standing between them and the enemy. They stand before their family in the sense of providing an example for them to see, providing a pre-standing example of godly character. They stand before them in the sense of leading and guiding in life (Heb 13:7). This clause of the text in Timothy does not itself deal with discipline, though many have read that idea in it. Discipline is good if it is in line with the biblical idea of fatherhood being one that stands before their children. The absent father, even for the sake of ministry, is contrary to ministry.

There is a blessing resulting in having children in subjection. This has to do with the end to which the children are being guided. It expounds on what it is to rightly rule or rule well. Paul would say to Titus, "If any be blameless, the husband of one wife, having faithful children not accused of riot or unruly" (Titus 1:6). The goal of the father is to have his children be obedient and submitted to Christ (2:11, II Cor 9:13). Comparing Timothy to Titus, these are faithful children, faithful to God and among those that are counted faithful. It is important because, again, this is the chief duty of a father (Eph 6:4). And then we have a noun in the genitive to tell us something of the quality of that subjection. Their children are subject "with all gravity." The word is translated honesty in the sense of having integrity and a tendency to not speak falsehoods. It is kin to the ideas of dignity, honor, or seriousness, describing the quality of one that should be held in reverence. Here the translators used the word gravity to describe someone that carries weight of character, someone of deep godly character. This is a blessing to all of society. The Psalmist, again spoke of faithful parentage as that which produces obedience, knowledge, and hope in generations following (Ps 78:1–10).

God has in this fractured world left a true point of unity from which blessings may flow in this world. It is worthy to be lauded by the saints and modeled by their leadership. God blessed the world through faithful Abraham, choosing him to bring a faithful seed into the world (Gen 12:1–3). He hedged this unity with the boundaries of the law. He has celebrated it by turning water into wine in its celebration (John 2:1–11). He has given us whole books about its redemption and its joy (Song of Solomon, Ruth, Esther, Hosea). He defined roles within it to strengthen its bulworks. He rebuked those who would forbid it (I Tim 4:1–4), those who would defile it (I Cor 5), and those that would put it asunder or separate it. God has declared His hatred for such things. He blessed it from the beginning and will rejoice in it to the end. The one true God who is unity and diversity loves the unity He blessed humanity with.

The Analogy of Sex

Synthesis 2: From the Marriage Bed
to the Marriage Supper

"Let us be glad and rejoice, and give honor to him: for the marriage of the Lamb is come, and his wife hath made herself ready."
Revelation 19:7

WE COME TO THE second, final, and most glorious synthesis. There is unity provided to us by God in this life as a common gift of His grace. That unity is found in marriage and its lasting good to all humanity as it exists in the boundaries of God's order. But there yet remains a unity and that unity can be found with God by a special work of His grace. This unity belongs to the redeemed of God and that grace we will call, in this treatise, reconciliation.

The fact that the first unity points to the second is an inherent truth of the Scriptures. Negatively, adultery was the most fitting description of idolatry. In the historical narrative, a marriage preceded the salvation of a people by God. Esther's marriage paved the way for the Jews as a nation to be saved from wrath and out of Ruth's marriage came not only the salvation of Naomi but the whole house of Elimelech and became the necessary preface for the covenant of David. The term redemption itself is indelibly connected with the practice of levirate marriage whereby entire families were ensured that their inheritance would not be lost. The Scriptures have bookends with marriage at its center. The beginning of the Scriptures is the creation and blessing of marriage and the end of the Scriptures is an invitation to an even greater marriage (Rev 22:17).

When solving the antitheses, we cannot stop at the existential fulfillment we find here and now. It is the greater fulfillment that makes the lesser analogy fulfilling. In other words, there is a deeper analogy to sex that speaks of a greater fulfillment and greater wholeness. Sex is pleasurable and fulfilling and marriage is a blessing that ripples through our generations, but it has its Creator that it should be leading us to That to which it points is the greater. We can express a thankfulness to our God for the lesser blessing, its pleasures, its fruit, its relationship building fellowship. But we cannot pretend like it is independent of Him. Nor can we pretend like any finite relationship can bring ultimate fulfillment. As great as sex is, it cannot give meaning or fulfillment in perfection. The time will come when those that have wives will be as those that have no wives. This world will pass away. The purposes of all earthly relationships will come to an end. There will come a point where we are no longer marrying or given in marriage (Matt 22:30).

Setting aside the termination of sexual reality, it is not possible that something less than a relationship with God can ever fulfill completely. Christian philosophers from Augustine to Pascal have strongly asserted that very truth. There is a greater relationship with your Lord and Creator that is central to our reality both here and now and for all eternity. We must know our God. Paul said that this was of the greatest importance. "But what things were gain to me, those I counted loss for Christ. Yea doubtless, and I count all things but loss for the excellency of the knowledge of Christ Jesus my Lord: for whom I have suffered the loss of all things, and do count them but dung, that I may win Christ . . . , That I may know him . . . " (Phil 3:7–11). In this sense, sex and marriage present us with a clue to a greater mystery, an analogy to a greater story.

Consider now the reality of the sexual relationship, the creation of human sexuality, and the covenant with which it was commenced as a theme to the greater end of God. There is, first, that which is separated from man, and then that which is reconciled back to man in the marriage covenant. The woman was taken from man to be returned in the covenant of marriage. Prior to the advent of sin, this covenant relationship was to be the source from which all blessings flow. Adam in receiving his bride embraced that which was bone of his bone and flesh of his flesh. He set it before the generations that were to come as a faithful remembrance of that first act. Others in the perpetuation of human history would leave their families to faithfully cleave unto their wives in unity. Sin then entered the world. The shame of nakedness came with it. The first thing Adam did after the judgment of God fell, after the promise of a Savior coming from the fruit of the woman's womb, but before God by grace alone covered the shame of their nakedness, was to look again to this covenant for ultimate hope (Gen 3:9–21). He looked to the woman and named her on the basis of the blessing that would yet come from her. When Adam looked in hope to that covenant, God responded by covering their shame. It was a beautiful picture of the greater need being fulfilled. In the reality of sin, man who had walked with God, being created in His very image, now stood apart from his God looking for reconciliation. And the theme of the marriage covenant is center stage now in the story of reconciliation.

There is far more to say than could possibly be said in this humble work. But I hope to provide a cursory outline here. Consider then the shadow of the covenant unity God had with man, prior to the advent of the sin. God as Lord is known to His people in terms of covenant. Covenant Theology is the approach to the Scriptures that sees the unfolding covenant realities in which the Lord God makes Himself known to His people as central to understanding the Scriptures. This is opposed to a dispensational understanding of biblical interpretation where God in capriciousness changes His relational dispositions toward man from time to time (though admittedly that is an incomplete understanding of such a view). To the covenant theologian God by grace relates Himself to His people through covenant. While there is much to say about the Lord/servant aspect of covenant, which was lightly touched on earlier when discussing antithesis, the covenant of marriage prior to the advent of Christ shows us that God intended to enter into a much more intimate relationship with His people. God spoke of His covenantal relationship with His people in terms of the marriage covenant and not just the Lord/servant relationship of the suzerain dynamic (i.e., the vassal relationship of a lesser state to a sovereign state).

Unfortunately, the covenant of marriage is tainted by the sinfulness of man, but it cannot be ignored as foreshadowing God's design of grace toward His elect. The foreshadowing is one of merciful love. God in this sense becomes known to us as the one that keeps mercy, or rather covenant love, with His people (Ex 34:7). And, even in the most extreme examples of the sin of His people, the keeping of this covenantal love leads to the truth that God saves His people from their sins (Matt 1:21).

The covenant of God with Israel was in terms of marriage. This is not so just with His covenant of law through Moses but also in the terms of promises given to Abraham when He called him out from his people. God describes this in the prophecy given by Ezekiel where, despite their heritage and poverty and sinfulness, "[God] looked upon thee, behold, thy time was the time of love; and I spread my skirt over thee, and covered thy nakedness: yea, I sware unto thee, and entered into a covenant with thee, saith the Lord God, and thou becamest mine" (Ezek 16:8). That is not a description of a Lord/servant relationship, but it is in the terms of the marriage covenant (Ruth 3:9). Ezekiel went on to describe God preparing Israel for Himself as a bride. However, they turned from the marriage covenant and committed fornication and adultery in utter unfaithfulness. The description of this unfaithfulness is hard to read. And God in His righteousness judged them in their idolatry. The judgment was severe. But the light of covenant love from a God that keeps mercy still shined through with the promise of a greater covenant yet to come. "I will even deal with thee as thou hast done, which hast despised the oath in breaking the covenant. Nevertheless I will remember my covenant with thee in the days of thy youth, and I will establish unto thee an everlasting covenant

. . . " (Ezek 16:59, 60). Any understanding of the new covenant of Christ must take this into an account as the greater act of love toward His sinful people. We can rejoice in His faithful love. "For thy Maker is thine husband; the Lord of hosts is his name; and thy Redeemer the Holy One of Israel; The God of the whole earth shall he be called . . . " (Isa 54:5).

When this aspect of covenant is seen in the Old Testament, it is hard to unsee in your reading of it. And in the Old covenant of law it highlights the holiness of God and as such highlights our greater need of grace as sinners. "For thou shalt worship no other god: for the Lord, whose name is Jealous, is a jealous God . . . " (Ex 34:14). Again, "For the Lord thy God is a consuming fire, even a jealous God" (Deut 4:24). God has an absolute right to our unwavering faithfulness toward Him, to worship and serve Him exclusively without any rival to our allegiance. He has the right of a husband in His covenant relationship with those to whom He has espoused Himself (II Cor 11:2). We have no right to take His name and live in any form of unfaithfulness to Him. Only a sexually perverted culture that has utterly embraced unfaithfulness and jettisoned any real concept of exclusivity in love can reject the idea of a jealous God. They know nothing of love. Our God is Jealous and righteously so. Thou shalt not have any other gods. He is to have no rival. His covenant name is what we have taken. And, in any honest assessment of ourselves, we are unfaithful (Jer 2:32, 3:20).

The law here is our schoolmaster (Gal 3:24, 25). Under the law, the presence of God judged whether or not one was faithful to their husband (Num 5). God knows. And God knows our unfaithfulness. Hosea tells this same story. Hosea is commanded by God to marry an unfaithful woman (Hosea 1). She goes forward and proves to be unfaithful. Hosea is told to put her away (Hos. 2:2). Other prophets also talked about God's just Bill of divorcement given to unfaithful Israel (Isa 50:1, Jer 3:8). But there stood yet the promise of grace in Hosea, "And I will betroth thee unto me for ever; yea, I will betroth thee unto me in righteousness, and in judgment, and in lovingkindness, and in mercies. I will even betroth thee unto me in faithfulness: and thou shalt know the LORD" (Hos 2:19, 20). The third chapter of Hosea leaves us with the reality of the old covenant and the hope of the new. The wife of Hosea was in chains on the auction block and was rescued by her faithful husband who promised to take her and her to be made faithful to him. And so the law took us as far it could in the love story of God for sinners. We are yet to be grafted into these promises.

The covenant unity was left incomplete in the Old covenant. It ended with Israel trying to rebuild their temple under the rule of foreign powers and still being rebuked for being unfaithful to their God by their prophets. But now we see another truth, foreshadowed from the beginning. The marriage covenant, under the terms of the law, left us all as adulterers before a faithful and just God (James 2: 10, 11, Rom 3:10–20). There is a natural and glorious tension in the law. The antithesis is clear. God will by no means clear the guilty. Yet God will keep mercy unto a thousand generations (Exo 34:6, 7). How will God bring unity to this? Paul's riddle was the same, how can God be just and the one that justifies the ungodly (Rom 3:26)? How can our Hosea justly put away her unfaithfulness and yet receive her forever as faithful? The Psalmist envisioned a day that righteousness and peace would kiss one another (Ps 85:10). But where is this synthesis, this reconciliation? God Himself pronounced its coming and did so in the reality of our unfaithfulness to His marriage covenant. "Behold, the days come, saith the Lord, that I will make a new covenant with the house of Israel, and with the house of Judah: Not according to the covenant that I made with their fathers in the day that I took them by the hand to bring them out of the land of Egypt; which my covenant they brake, although I was an husband unto them, saith the Lord: But this shall be the covenant that I will make with the house of Israel; After those days, saith the Lord, I will put my law in their inward parts, and write it in their hearts; and will be their God, and they shall be my people" (Jer 31:31–33). The answer is clear, grace, free grace from God. It will be done by God, just as the first marriage back in the garden.

But, on what basis can a good God save those over whom the threat of death looms? What hope does the adulterer have under the law. The adulterer is under the righteous sentence of death (Deut 22:22-24)? The covenant of marriage was the last prophecy given before the fall (Gen 2:23, 24). The first prophecy after the fall was the promise of one that was coming that would destroy the work of sin that wrought the fall (Gen 3:15). It was God's answer of grace to man's sin. The first prophecy was that a "man" would leave His father and mother to cleave to His wife. And the second prophecy was that a man would come, the seed of the woman, to bruise the head of tempter. Prophecy under the old covenant from Job to Jeremiah, from the tabernacle to the second temple, from Moses to Isaiah, looked for this coming hero and redeemer. This salvation would come from God, but the marriage covenant demanded that it be of man, bone of his bone and flesh of his flesh. Nothing else in creation could come along man's side for his help. God would lay our help on one that is mighty (Ps 89:19).

The answer to the synthesis is the incarnation of Christ. He was God and was with God in the beginning (John 1:1-3). And He was made flesh and dwelt among us (John 1:14). It was fitting that He partook in our flesh that He might be our merciful help (Heb 2:14-18). Paul, when expounding the great mystery of Christ revealed to us, spoke in terms of the marriage covenant. As the woman was brought out of the side of Adam, a humanity made new was brought forth from Christ. The people of God are His bone and His flesh and His mission to faithfully be united to. "For we are members of his body, of his flesh, and of his bones. For this cause shall a man leave his father and mother, and shall be joined unto his wife, and they two shall be one flesh. This is a great mystery: but I speak concerning Christ and the church" (Eph 5:30-32). Christ brought the unity that could not be brought by the law (Rom 8:1-4). This is what made the prophecy of Hosea a reality. Here the God/Man seeks sinful man, sinful man proving unworthy, and God by grace alone keeps covenant. The new covenant is all about what God (the God/man) did to redeem His people.

Reconciliation with God comes from the obedient life and sacrificial death of Christ for all who are in Christ, just as separation from God came to all represented by Adam in his disobedience (Rom 5:12–21). This unity is a present reality to the church of God. Christ has given us peace with God, access to God, rejoicing in this world of tribulation, and an abounding experience of the love of God by His presence among us (Rom 5:1–5). We are those who walk with God in this world (Rom 8:1). Again, we are called to faithfulness in body and spirit for we are the temple of God and the Spirit of God is in us individually and among us corporately (I Cor 3:16). We enjoy the intimate leadership and protection of our Head, "Christ is the head of the church: and he is the savior of the body" (Eph 5:23). We bask in His loving sacrifice for us, "Husbands, love your wives, even as Christ also loved the church, and gave himself for it . . . " (Eph 5:25). And we are subject to His acts of ministry as He sets us apart for Himself and prepares us now to be received forever in His abiding; "That he might sanctify and cleanse it with the washing of water by the word, That he might present it to himself a glorious church, not having spot, or wrinkle, or any such thing; but that it should be holy and without blemish" (Eph 5:26, 27).

We are presently being prepared for the end of all things, the marriage supper where we will enter forever into the Father's house, into the dwelling prepared for us by Christ (John 14:1–6). The bride of Christ will one day be received by Christ in her white robes (Rev 21). The plot which was set by God in the first marriage covenant will be brought to fullness when the church goes out to meet her Lord. A marriage supper will one day be had. The bride is making herself ready by the grace of Christ. One day the cry will be heard that the bridegroom comes. The invitation has gone out to all to be a part of that day. And when it comes, those that are His will forever be with Him (I Thess 4:16–18).

Conclusion

The Blessing of Sex

Thesis: Human Sexuality is a Good Gift from the Blessed God

"Every good gift and every perfect gift is from above, and cometh down from the Father of lights, with whom is no variableness, neither shadow of turning." James 1:17

A WORD OR TWO is needed to bring this matter to a conclusion. Under the umbrella of antithesis, it was noted that all necessary distinctions that arise regarding sex are put forth by God as Lord of all. He created human sexuality specifically with all its distinctions. We must rightly judge sex in the light of those clear distinctions in order for it not to become matter for our judgment. We must seek the greater things of God and rightly reject what is not of Him. Under the umbrella of synthesis, it was noted that the necessary distinctions that must be made do not contradict the underlying unity God has attached to human sexuality. There is a wholeness found in the husband/wife relationship and it is a fitting analogy for the wholeness and unity we find with God through Christ, both now and forever.

In a world that ignores the necessary antithesis, the temptation is to assert truths of God that tend to legalize the subject of sex. This leaves a view of sex that is sterile and lacks vitality, a list of prohibitions that leave the reality of it cold and lifeless. In a world

SEX AND THE GOSPEL

that is ignorant of the synthesis intended by sex, the temptation is to accommodate the evil world by legitimizing those things that cannot bring wholeness (i.e., immorality). This saps the virtue from sex and turns it into a passing empty pleasure.

The Biblical thesis then is this, that sex as it is given by God is a source of great blessing to mankind and leads us to praise the blessed God who pours out such blessings upon us. Solomon said, "Whoso findeth a wife findeth a good thing, and obtaineth favor of the Lord" (Prov 18:22). God intended for that to be the experience of Adam and continues to intend it to be a reality for all.

Throughout these musings, my sincere hope is that we have seen these truths. The covenant of marriage and all that it produces in the will of God has blessed mankind. A wife is blessed by God when she has a husband who seeks to love her and honor her. The husband is blessed when he has a wife who is wise and prudent and serves in virtue. "A prudent wife *is* from the LORD" (Prov 19:14). Children are blessed by having parents who teach them the fear of God and nurture them in instruction (Eph 6:1–5). Society as a whole is blessed to have this as its underlying structure. Human sexuality as given by God brings forth generations of those who know, fear, and hope in God (Ps 78:1–10). Marriage is a setting for Christ to be intimately shown in our relationships. It sanctifies the most intimate details of our lives and gives us a place of inexhaustible and meaningful service. It enriches our lives and prepares us for greater service. It shows us a world yet to be where we will be with our Lord, a partaker of His joy, forever.

www.ingramcontent.com/pod-product-compliance
Lightning Source LLC
Chambersburg PA
CBHW060311100426
42812CB00003B/748